EVERYWOMAN'S MONEY™

Confident Investing

by Deborah Owens

*Kathryn :)
Expect big things !
to happen !
Debbie O*

alpha books
201 West 103rd Street
Indianapolis, IN 46290

A Pearson Education Company

International Standard Book Number: 0-02-864010-1
Library of Congress Catalog Card Number: Available from the Library of Congress.

03   02   01   8 7 6 5 4 3 2 1

Interpretation of the printing code: The rightmost number of the first series of numbers is the year of the book's printing; the rightmost number of the second series of numbers is the number of the book's printing. For example, a printing code of 01-1 shows that the first printing occurred in 2001.

Printed in the United States of America

ALPHA BOOKS

PUBLISHER:
Marie Butler-Knight

PRODUCT MANAGER:
Phil Kitchel

MANAGING EDITOR:
Jennifer Chisholm

ACQUISITIONS EDITOR:
Mike Sanders

DEVELOPMENT EDITOR:
Michael Thomas

SENIOR PRODUCTION EDITOR:
Christy Wagner

COPY EDITOR:
Amy Lepore

COVER DESIGNER:
Anne Jones

BOOK DESIGNER:
Trina Wurst

INDEXER:
Lisa Wilson

LAYOUT/PROOFREADING:
John Etchison
Mark Walchle

EVERYWOMAN'S COMPANY

EXECUTIVE PROJECT DIRECTOR:
Jan Black

MANAGING PROJECT DIRECTOR:
Joseph Roberts

CONTRIBUTING EDITOR:
Diana Williams

Contents

Foreword

The *Everywoman's Money™* series is one more expression of the Everywoman vision to educate and empower women to fund the lives they want to live, and to create and sustain financial well-being. These books, and all other Everywoman's Money™ products and events, are rooted in this mission.

Through the creation and presentation of the Everywoman's Money™ Conferences around the country, women are telling us what they want to know and how they want it explained. Women know their need to be money-smart is more essential than ever. They are emerging with new levels of assets, responsibilities, and opportunities, requiring them to have a thorough knowledge of how money works.

Just as they are experiencing new opportunities, women also continue to be challenged by some very real financial risks. At this writing, two thirds of America's poor are women, many of whom lived middle-class lives until a divorce or death of a husband sent them into poverty. Eighty-five percent of the elderly poor are women, and 100,000 of the 127,000 people over 100 years of age are, you guessed it, women. Collectively, women still earn only 75 percent of what men earn, and their in-and-out careers (because of caring for children and parents) produce smaller pensions. In other words, women in general have less money available than men to sustain a life that lasts longer than men's.

Women must compensate for this shortfall by getting smart about money and how it grows so they can have enough for long enough. This is why Everywoman's Money™ exists. It is why we are committed to "teaching money like it's never been taught before."

Jan Black
Jody Temple-White

Founders, The Everywoman's Company and Project Green Purse

Introduction

As I prepared to write this introduction, I happened upon a picture of my mother and four of her sisters. It was taken in the 1950s in a nightclub; they were sitting at a table looking like movie stars, all dolled up in fitted black dresses. The first time I saw this picture I didn't recognize my mother. That picture allowed me to see her as a vibrant, beautiful woman with a full life ahead and not just my mother. Like so many women of her day she sacrificed for others and took on roles that did not always benefit her economically. After attending one of the Everywoman's Money™ Conferences she commented, "The chains and shackles are being taken off of women by their learning how to take care of themselves financially." Those words are my reason for writing this book.

Women's incomes have increased significantly in the past twenty years, and yet at this writing there are new statistics indicating that two thirds of women age 55 and older live in poverty. *Everywoman's Money™: Confident Investing* will provide you with the tools you need to create a life of abundance.

Each chapter begins with a woman's story and provides you with a real-life example of the challenges you may face as you begin your financial journey. These women changed my life as we faced their challenges, and they can change yours, too. All of the women had to take control of their finances and learn how to create wealth for themselves. You can be financially empowered, too! Let the women in this book become your money mentors. If you haven't had anyone to show you how to invest, then consider these stories a gift. Use these experiences as your model for financial success. Apply the lessons they learned to your own situation. At the end of each chapter, you should capture your thoughts and ideas by writing them down in the "Reader's Journal" area that we have provided. As you identify specific steps and actions, your financial plan will begin to formulate. Look at this book as your personal guide to investing with confidence.

Everywoman's Money™: Confident Investing begins by addressing some of the common issues that women face financially. We earn less, save less, and can be uncomfortable making decisions with our money that involve risk. It's important to understand what the barriers to success are in order to move beyond them. Each subsequent chapter covers investment concepts that you need to understand in order to make informed and critical decisions about investing. We recognize that financial terms and concepts are sometimes difficult to digest and have provided you with a "money coach" and "money therapist" to assist you with the right-brain issues that are often forgotten in books about investing. We've tried to anticipate the unique needs of women as investors. But at the end of the day, all of this information means absolutely nothing unless you do something with it. Do! Act! Be!

How This Book Is Organized

True to the Everywoman's Money™ brand, these books, and those that will follow, address specific financial topics with a particular personality and holistic tone that is smart, respectful, punchy, and warm.

Each *Everywoman's Money™* book is organized to include:

Everywoman Stories

When you attend an Everywoman's Money™ Conference, you will meet Everywomen whose stories are told on video periodically throughout the day. Each chapter of these books opens with similar stories of real women. You will learn from them and apply their experiences to your own.

Coaching Tips

Karen Sheridan, our Everywoman's Money™ Coach at live events, is also your financial coach in these books. Karen is beloved for her frankness, humor, and passion for helping women like you master money. She owns her own money-management company in the Northwest.

Money Therapy

Olivia Mellan, Money Therapist and popular speaker at Everywoman's Money™ events, accompanies you as you read the books through an ongoing commentary called "Money Therapy." Olivia presents the psychology side of money. She is noted for her groundbreaking work in identifying money personalities.

Reader's Journal and Assessments

For readers who want to record what they have learned and the steps they want to take, there are journal entry pages at the end of each chapter. Throughout the books, there are also places for the reader to complete helpful financial assessments and information.

Glossary

A glossary of terms related to the title of each book is included to help you talk the topic.

Acknowledgments

This book would not have been possible if not for the tireless efforts of several people. First, a special thanks to my husband, Terry, and children, Brandon and Olivia, who allowed me to write without feeling guilty about missing their soccer games, swim meets, and other events. My sincere thanks to Joan Coulahan and Sue Van Derlinden, Everywoman's Empowerment Team members, who weighed in and contributed their expertise on investing for women. A special note of gratitude to Joseph Roberts, whose expertise, judgment, and wisdom was the glue that held this ambitious project together. And to Diana, who assisted with the background research and editing needed to make the book complete. This was truly a collaborative effort. Jan Black, founder of the Everywoman's Company, was the tireless champion of it all. She wrote, cajoled, and encouraged everyone with her sense of urgency and tenacity to get the job done. Without her vision, the first series of books dedicated to women and money would not be.

I would also like to thank editors Michael Thomas and Christy Wagner at Alpha Books for making absolutely sure that the ideas being conveyed in this book are easily understood.

Trademarks

Erma was the daughter of a farmer and the fifth of 12 children. Life on the farm in the 1940s was harsh, backbreaking work. Erma and thousands of young women like her saw marriage as the only way out.

At 17, Erma caught sight of a confident young man carrying a briefcase and promising to travel the world. With only three months left before her high school graduation, Erma married him and left home.

True to his word, he traveled the world with Erma during his term in the Navy. He eventually settled into a job with an airline; Erma gave birth to five children. When her youngest started school, Erma went to work in an automobile factory. With combined incomes, the family was solidly middle class and enjoyed vacations, a modest but nice home, and the belief that the future would always be the same.

Erma was in her tenth year at the factory when her husband chose to pursue his dream of living in Hawaii. She and the kids went with him. A few years later, without her own checking account or any established credit of her own, Erma left her husband. She was no longer middle class—but impoverished.

Twenty years later, Erma survives each month on Social Security, a $100 pension from the auto factory, and support from her children.

Chapter 1

Why Investing Is Essential

The Bottom Line

Investing is no longer an option if you want to retain control of your choices now and for life.

Erma is my mother. As her child, I have lived her choices, as my children are living mine. As a young girl, I adopted her belief that having a man and having financial security were one and the same. I was liberated from that belief the day my parents separated.

I was 18 and about to enter college. My mother was living in one of the most expensive parts of the country, suddenly having to support herself and quickly spiraling into poverty. I vowed to never depend on anyone to support me. And I promised myself that I would get smart about money.

My experience and promise to myself were what drove me to become a stockbroker. They are also what drive me to help women take control of their financial lives.

Realities

My mother's story is not unusual. And it is not limited to women over 70. To some degree, most of us hold beliefs about roles and money that limit and endanger us financially. It's time to get past them and move into a place where men and women take personal responsibility for their financial success.

We women know how to get a job done. Our brains are wired for doing many things at once. Investing was made for our kind of thinking. It's fast, it's moving, it takes some planning, we can prepare it now and pick it up later, it's interesting, and it makes for good conversation—that is, if we would just start talking about it.

If we're so amazing, why have so many of us hesitated to invest? I think the answer to that question lies in how we view wealth and success. For many women, me included, making financial decisions puts us in conflict with the world's perception of us. Isn't the stock market a man's domain? Shouldn't we wait for someone to give us permission? If I get smart at investing, will I seem like less of a woman?

These questions seem outdated, but then, so is our hesitancy to invest. Deferring our financial decision-making to a man (a spouse, father, brother, adviser) is still the picture that many of us have. We must erase it or erase our chances at a life that holds good things for us and those we love.

Changing our perception of ourselves is the first step toward becoming more confident about investing. Wall Street may have been designed by men for men, but money doesn't care whether you are male or female. Invest it wisely, and it will grow for you.

Your life depends on how well you invest. Sound scary? It is. Despite the gains that women have made in our society, we are still more likely to live in poverty at retirement than men. In fact, women comprise 85 percent of the elderly poor.

Despite the significant strides that we have made in the workforce, we are still likely to have to depend on our children or a relative to take care of us later in life. This alone is motivation to build enough wealth to stay in charge of our lives to the end.

The real game of chance is to not invest and still expect to have enough money to live as you hope you will.

As you can see from the following "Sources of Retirement Income" chart, you will need an assortment of income streams to successfully complete your life with enough money. Social Security was never meant to be a person's sole retirement income. Yet most women in poverty rely on it to live. Most of these women lived middle-class lives before their retirement years.

Sources of Retirement Income

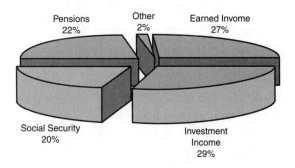

Sources of retirement income.

If Erma had known then what she knows today, she would have done things differently:

- ❖ She would not have mistaken love and marriage for financial security.
- ❖ She would not have limited her career choices by limiting her education.
- ❖ She would have established a purse of her own.
- ❖ She would have put money away for her retirement when she was a young mother.
- ❖ She would not have sacrificed her own future financial needs and quality of life.

Fortunately for you and me, we live in a new day of women and money, and as women, we are collectively opening the door for one another to a new way of protecting ourselves and our children from poverty and limited choices.

Erma Would Tell You to Invest

Today, Erma emphatically believes in investing. She has learned from my work and wishes that she had known the power of investing a long time ago. If Erma were sitting with you today, she would urge you to invest.

Erma would tell you that investing can ...

❖ Protect you from being a financial victim.

❖ Give you control over your choices.

❖ Permit you to pursue the work and pleasure that is best for you.

❖ Give you the economic power to decide where to live and what to buy.

❖ Set the stage for your children to invest and reap the benefits.

A Key to Taking Control

Investing helps you take control of your financial future. This is not an anti-male perspective. Rather, it is a pro-everyone perspective. Each person must be responsible for her or his own financial well-being, even when in a happy relationship.

Life tosses us some unexpected opportunities and tragedies. As Teresa Wilhelmi, keyboard improv artist at Everywoman's Money™ Conferences, says, "The reason I can play improv at the piano is because I know the fundamentals of this keyboard." She adds, "As you learn the fundamentals of money and investing, you will be able to play well what life hands you financially."

Money Therapy

If you aren't used to sitting down and having regular "moneytalks" with your partner—and I recommend doing this monthly at least—then begin by finding a relaxed time to talk. Consider sharing the messages about money you received in childhood and how they might be affecting you now. Neither partner should interrupt or judge the other during this fragile process. Finally, after sharing your feelings, fears, hopes, and dreams, with each partner listening respectfully, you should be ready to move on to the hard facts of your money life.

Olivia Mellan

The reality that women have avoided is this: Money is power. We don't like the word *power* because we often think of it as domination.

But in this case, *power* means authority—authority to make choices about your life and your future. Karen McCall, author of *It's Your Money* and pioneer in the work of financial recovery, often cites a speech by Nelson Mandela that says we are afraid of our own power and light. He calls us to release our power and greatness so that all can benefit. I call on you to release your power financially so that all can benefit.

Money adds weight to your opinions and increases your influence. For example, if I didn't have my own financial assets, my husband, Terry, would have had a much different response to career choices that I've made. Because I do have my own assets, in addition to those we have together, I am able to choose what I do in my work and how I do it. I value and seek his opinion, as he does mine, but I have the freedom and voice to chart my course—because I have money in my pocket.

As tough as it is to say, all decisions in our lives really come down to money. Investing can help you acquire more money and therefore give you more control over your life.

Best Chance to Have Enough

Investing keeps you moving ahead financially instead of stalling. If your money is standing still, you're falling behind. The cost of things that you need and want is going up every day. If your money isn't being invested so that it creates more money and enables you to keep up, the money that you have will not be enough for what you need and want.

Investing is your best chance to have enough to …

- ❖ Make career moves that are good for you.
- ❖ Start your own business.
- ❖ Contribute to your parents' lives, if you choose, without it being a burden.
- ❖ Send your kids to college.
- ❖ Go to college yourself.
- ❖ Stop working for a salary and work for personal enjoyment instead.
- ❖ Pursue your dreams, not just a paycheck.

Women generally live longer than men. Someone must pay for your care in your later years. If you have the money to make the choice, you'll choose to live in quality. If you don't, someone else will choose who will care for you and where. Investing can help you have enough to live the way you want to at the end of your life.

You Will Face Life Changes

You've lived long enough to know that life is unpredictable. We go into it believing that we have control over almost everything in our lives, and then it happens—a surprise that lights our fire or rocks our boat. We win an award, we get fired, our parents split, friends take us on a cruise, the college that we chose doesn't choose us, we have twins, companies go under, the biopsy is positive, or our car insurance wasn't renewed after all.

As women, 90 percent of us will be solely in charge of our finances at some point in our lives. This means that we will experience life changes. We will marry, probably more than once, have children, survive our partner, or be responsible for the care of a parent or relative.

Not only that, but we also will evolve as people with passions that surface and beg for expression. We will want the money to go to New Mexico on a photographic mission. We will want to contribute time and money to the outdoor camp for troubled kids that helped our grandchild.

Facing life changes is easier with enough money. Investing can help you have enough.

You Will Need More Than You Think

You know how it is when you plan a vacation or remodel a room. It nearly always costs more than you thought it would. Even more certain, living your life—even a life of simplicity—will cost more than you think it will. Investing keeps your money growing so that you can keep up with rising costs.

Not only are costs of today's products increasing, but breakthroughs in medicine and technology also are producing incredible products that will enhance and improve our lives. You'll want enough money to benefit from them.

So, my message to you is that you'll need more money than you think you will to live, give, and love well for the rest of your life.

Every Woman Must Invest

Yesterday I was at a bus stop with a couple that lives near us. From previous conversations, I had learned that he had a Roth IRA. I asked the wife if she had opened a Roth IRA. She said that she hadn't because she didn't work. I said to her husband, "You can open a Roth IRA for your wife and contribute $2,000 even if she has no income, you know." He said, "Well, it would have to come out of our family budget, so, no, I haven't."

This reminded me again that as women, we must insist on being financially protected, in our names, and that even those who love us don't naturally think to do it. It is our responsibility, no one else's.

Soon after our conversation, the neighbor did open a Roth IRA for his wife. It isn't that he didn't want his wife protected; he just didn't think that it was important enough to use family money to do it. He was buying into the myth that she would automatically be taken care of and that women somehow don't need the same retirement money that men do, even though most women outlive their husbands. (We'll discuss how to invest for retirement in Chapter 13, "Investing for Retirement.")

Just as investing is no longer a choice, it is no longer a mystery. Anyone can do it, and investing can be done on as little as $25 a month. Investing is becoming mainstream, an established societal habit, like exercise.

Unlike Erma, you and I have access to any information about investing that we want. Old limitations that we as women used to face are being lifted, and we're finding out that we are quite competent investors. Free classes on investing are offered in nearly every city, and the Internet is becoming a woman's best tool for finding specific information and taking action.

Myths

I've told you that I adopted my mother's belief that having a man meant having financial security. There are other myths that keep us from investing and taking control of our financial lives:

- ❖ **Investing is a man's game.** Most games are now open to both genders, including investing. An incredible rise in investment clubs for women proves that investing is everyone's game. Join in.

❖ **Investing is difficult.** It's not as hard as you think—otherwise, people who aren't as smart as you wouldn't be doing it.

❖ **Investing is for the rich.** Not anymore. It's for those who want to be rich, too.

❖ **Investing is too risky.** When someone says this to me, I ask her to choose her fear. Would she rather fear losing money in something like the stock market, which has an outstanding record of making money over time? Or would she rather fear that her money, sitting in a low-interest bank account, will lose the battle against inflation? There's risk either way.

❖ **Investing takes too long to bring returns.** You invest for the long term, even though there are often short-term gains. It's your future that you're investing in. You're preparing for your life later. Of course, this doesn't mean that there aren't ways to benefit from your investments sooner.

If you hold on to these myths, you'll be stalled on your path to financial well-being. By waiting to invest, you are giving away the most important thing you need to be successful at investing: time.

Erma would put it to you straighter than I just did. She would tell you that these aren't myths. They're excuses.

Challenges

The challenges of investing are only as big as you let them be. You can surmount them in 15 minutes, 4 years, a lifetime, or never. It's your choice.

❖ **Decide to begin.** The fear of embarking upon the unknown is natural, but we do it all the time. You may or may not be around people who invest, and stepping beyond what your circle of friends and family do can be frightening. Do it anyway. Everyone will benefit from your courage.

❖ **Learn what you need to know.** As we said before, there has never been more information about investing; it comes in every form imaginable, from books to Web sites to classes to clubs.

❖ **Get started.** Start where you are, with what you have, even if it's $25 a month or $10 a week. Keep it simple—just do it.

Coaching Tip

When you know how money works, you become confident. You know how to manage your money, and you *know* that you know. It makes a big difference in your life.

You only have to learn it once. Then build on what you know. Before long, you're an expert.

The Bottom Line

Moving past your personal investment myths and challenges and into confident investing will put you in the best position for meeting the opportunities and responsibilities that you assume as a woman. Investing is no longer a mystery—or an option.

Reader's Journal:

Knowledge Gained:

_____

_____

_____

_____

_____

_____

_____

_____

_____

_____

Steps I Will Take:

_____

_____

_____

_____

_____

_____

_____

_____

_____

_____

At 40-something, Ida decided that it was time to get serious about her money life. She was recently divorced and doing her best to help her daughter and grandchildren financially. She was a social worker, employed by the government most of her career.

Ida was a saver who had recently awakened to the idea of investing. She liked the idea of money making money. Until then, she had chosen the "guaranteed" options on her employer's retirement plan, but now she was opening up to something more daring but still considered safe.

Ida had a skepticism about financial professionals that many women share, yet she wanted to learn how to invest. She decided that she would learn all she could on her own and then visit a financial adviser. That's when I met her.

Ida frequently called my radio show and eventually hired me to present a seminar to her colleagues at work. Since then, she has constructed her own investment portfolio and accumulated a portfolio of several thousand dollars that includes stocks, mutual funds, and IRAs.

She has also helped her daughter begin an investment program to save for her grandchildren's college education. Not only that, but Ida recently presented a workshop on socially responsible investing at a recent convention.

Ida found her way from where she was to where she wanted to be. If she were standing in a mall at the store directory, she would look for the red "You Are Here" circle. Then she would look for the store that she wanted to visit and determine the path to take based on the other stores on her list and how much time and energy she had.

In effect, that's what she did financially. She figured out where she was, decided where she wanted to be, and created a path to get there based on her own style, experience, money, and plans. Then she followed the path and arrived at her destination.

Ida did it her way. You can do it your way.

Chapter 2

Here You Are

The Bottom Line

When you know where you are and where you want to be, it's easy to connect the dots to get there.

Where are you on the path to investing? Whether you're a non-investor or an experienced one, there are things to learn and places to go. Investing is a fascinating endeavor at every stage.

Where You Are

I've built this chapter around an illustrated directional tool created by Everywoman's Money called the "Where You Are" grid. It's a simple, effective way to help you see where you are, where you want to be, and what you want to know. (The answer to

"How will I get there once I know?" will be developed into your personal plan as each chapter is completed.)

The process centers on investing, not your money profile at large, and clarifies where you are with regard to money you want to invest, knowledge you have about investing, access you have to investment guidance and tools, confidence you have about investing, and your determination to become a competent investor.

Here is what you do:

1. Read each of the following sections.
2. Mark the statements as indicated in each section.
3. Add up your number of yes answers and place an X in the corresponding square.

This is not a test and certainly is not a measurement of your ability to invest. It's more like a compass that gives you direction about your next steps.

I've included sample grids as Ida might have completed them before she became an investor (see the following pages).

This "Where You Are" grid, like Ida's, will show you where you are in relation to money, knowledge, accessibility, confidence, and determination. Complete it step by step as you finish the chapter.

Where You Are
Ida's First Grid

	Money	Knowledge	Accessibility	Confidence	Determination
7					
6			X		X
5	X				
4					
3					
2				X	
1		X			
0					

Ida's first grid.

Where You Are
Ida's After Six Months

	Money	Knowledge	Accessibility	Confidence	Determination
7					X
6	X		X		
5		X		X	
4					
3					
2					
1					
0					

Ida after six months.

Where You Are with Money

Money is not only the starting point, it's also the end point of investing, so let's begin here. Where are you with regard to money and investing?

Ida was already a saver who participated in her company's retirement plan, but initially in the most conservative way. Because she was very conscious of her money, she would have answered "yes" to most of these questions. What will your answers be?

1. Do you spend less than you earn? Y N
2. Do you save some each month? Y N
3. Do you currently invest? Y N
4. Do you participate in your company's retirement plan? Y N
5. Do you max your contribution to the plan? Y N
6. If you don't have access to a company retirement plan, do you invest in an IRA or other tax-advantaged investment? Y N
7. Do you have enough cash put away to cover expenses for three to six months, if necessary? Y N

The great part of investing is that if you are short on the amount of money you need—say, for a six-month emergency fund—investing can help you earn the money to build the fund. If you are far from matching the money profile outlined here, don't be ashamed or embarrassed. You can catch up more easily than you think—especially when you invest.

Now count your "yes" answers and place a dot on the grid in the
Money column where you believe you are, based on your answers.

Where You Are in Knowledge

Knowledge is a key element in confident investing. How much do you
know about investing?

Ida not only didn't know about investing, she didn't *want* to know.
Over time, information gradually seeped into her mind and motivated
her to rethink her position. She liked the idea of her money making
more money, and she launched her own campaign to learn about
investing.

While Ida would have said "yes" to most of the questions about
money, she would have scored nearly a zero on those about knowledge. This proves that each person's path to investing is unique—a
message that I want to emphasize.

Where are you in your knowledge of investing? Here are some questions to help you figure out what you know and don't know. Answer
these questions, and then place a dot on the grid in the Knowledge
column in the place that most accurately represents your level of
knowledge.

1. Do you know how to create a net worth statement? Y N
2. Do you know how to track a stock's performance? Y N
3. Do you understand your time horizons? Y N
4. Do you understand the difference between stocks, bonds, and
   mutual funds? Y N
5. Do you understand your risk tolerance? Y N
6. Do you know how to research a company whose stock you may
   want to buy? Y N
7. Do you understand asset allocation? Y N

Ida went from not knowing anything about investing to leading seminars on it. No matter what you don't know, you can learn it quickly.
In fact, if you didn't know anything from the previous list, you could
learn all of it in a matter of days. Take it from Ida: Anyone can learn
to invest, and this book will help you do it.

Where Are You with Accessibility?

By "accessibility," I mean, how easily can you get the information you need?

Ida didn't want to get her information from financial professionals at first, so she learned what she needed to know in other ways.

Identify where you are with regard to accessibility. Answer these questions, and place a dot in the Accessibility column on your grid in the place that most accurately represents the number of "yes" answers you gave.

1. Do you have a computer or wireless device with Internet access? Y N
2. Do you have a television and/or radio? Y N
3. Do you know a financial professional? Y N
4. Do you bank at a local bank or credit union? Y N
5. Do you have a friend or family member who invests? Y N
6. Do you subscribe to a newspaper or magazine? Y N
7. Do you have a library or bookstore in your community? Y N

It's revealing to see a list like this and realize how accessible investment information has become. From this pool of information, Ida taught herself to invest. Whether you choose to teach yourself or take advantage of direct investment training by a professional, the resources are all around you.

Confidence

After Ida decided to invest, she was confident that she could learn to do it because she had mastered other things in her life that had seemed difficult at first. No matter where you are in the learning curve of investing—a beginner or a woman who wants to increase her investment savvy—confidence will play a big role in your success.

Identify where you are with regard to confidence.

1. Are you able to hear news of the market dropping without feeling a sense of panic? Y N
2. When a new investment opportunity becomes available, do you explore it? Y N
3. Do you talk with others about the subject of investing? Y N

4. Do you educate yourself about investing? Y N

5. Do you easily ask questions of financial professionals? Y N

6. Do you actively participate in investment decisions? Y N

7. Are you able to receive advice and then decide on your own whether to follow it? Y N

Place a dot in the Confidence column on your grid in the place that most accurately represents the level of confidence you have.

Money Therapy

Whatever step you take, I call this "practicing the nonhabitual" in my money harmony work. When you do something that doesn't come naturally, it builds new capacities and gives you an expanded sense of self-confidence and self-esteem.

Olivia Mellan

Determination

It's possible to be confident but not determined, and it's also possible to be determined but not confident. Without determination, you will not move to the next level of investing because you'll find reasons not to do it.

Ida was determined to learn to invest because she wanted her money to make more money. This would improve her life and the life of the people she loved. Once she caught sight of the possibilities, she was determined to grab them.

Identify where you are with regard to determination.

1. Are you willing to adjust your spending habits in order to invest? Y N

2. Are you willing to adjust your saving habits in order to invest? Y N

3. Are you willing to spend time to learn about investing? Y N

4. Are you willing to do what's necessary to step past your fear of investing? Y N

5. Are you willing to weather the ups and downs of the market long term? Y N

6. Are you willing to set aside short-term gratification for long-term gain? Y N

7. Are you willing to acknowledge what you don't know in order to get where you want to be? Y N

Place a dot in the Determination column on your grid in the place that most accurately represents the level of determination you have.

Here You Are

Now look at your grid to see where you are in your current relationship to investing. My friend Jennifer looked at her grid and saw that the only thing she was low in was money. At first this discouraged her because she believed that she had everything but what she really needed to invest—money! I helped her "find" money in her existing pattern of spending, and she quickly stepped into the world of investing as an investor herself.

Sheila, on the other hand, looked at her grid and saw that she was low in everything but determination. As you can imagine, her situation quickly changed because determination is an ingredient that moves us forward, regardless of the obstacles.

Now that you've stood at the store directory in the mall, so to speak, and found the dot that shows you where you are in relationship to investing, it's time to find where you want to be.

 Coaching Tip

Start with pencil and paper. Write everything down. If you have a written plan, you're well on your way. Once you have a plan, the rest is just editing as your life circumstances change and as the years go by.

Where You Want to Be

Using the following grids, show where you want to be in six months and one year.

Where You Want to Be (in Six Months)

	Money	Knowledge	Accessibility	Confidence	Determination
7					
6					
5					
4					
3					
2					
1					
0					

"Where You Want to Be" grid (six months).

Where You Want to Be (in One Year)

	Money	Knowledge	Accessibility	Confidence	Determination
7					
6					
5					
4					
3					
2					
1					
0					

"Where You Want to Be" grid (one year).

Now you know where you are and where you want to be. Take a few more minutes to determine what you want to know.

What You Want to Know

You might be a person who decides that she wants to know everything there is to know about investing. Or, you might just want to know how to fit investing into your busy life. It's helpful to determine what you want to know at this time so that you can acquire the knowledge and move on.

Read the topics of knowledge here, and mark their order of priority to you on the "What You Want to Know" grid.

1. How investing is done
2. How the stock market works

3. How to fit investing into your life

4. How to find trusted advice

5. How to select investment products

6. How to keep track of stocks and the stock market

7. How your investment gains/losses affect your taxes

8. How to begin

9. How to advance to the next level of investing

10. Other

What You Want to Know

What You Want to Know	Order of Priority
1. How investing is done	
2. How the stock market works	
3. How to fit investing into your life	
4. How to find trusted advice	
5. How to select investment products	
6. How to keep track of stocks and the stock market	
7. How your investment gains/losses affect your taxes	
8. How to begin	
9. How to advance to the next level of investing	
10. Other:	

"What You Want to Know" grid.

There You Go

You've seen where you are, and you've chosen where you want to go and what you want to learn. This is important information to have; now you have a path and a direction of your own.

Ida would tell you to get going. So would every woman who invests, including me.

The Bottom Line

If you know where you are and where you want to go, you can get there.

Reader's Journal:

Knowledge Gained:

_____

_____

_____

_____

_____

_____

_____

_____

_____

_____

Steps I Will Take:

_____

_____

_____

_____

_____

_____

_____

_____

_____

_____

Three years ago, Cara didn't know the difference between a stock and a mutual fund. Now she not only knows the difference, but she's also profiting from it and on her way to creating a very special life.

After graduating from college, Cara landed a job as a producer of a talk show. One year later, she became an associate producer at a mid-sized-market television station. Now, two years later, she is the director of public affairs for the same station and often finds herself meeting with top politicians and newsmakers in her state.

Cara's job is stimulating and exciting, yet she dreams of leaving it to spend her time traveling and pursuing other interests. She's well on her way to achieving that dream because the choices that she makes today are driven by the goal that she has to retire at 45.

How will she do it? Cara saves more than 30 percent of her income. She contributes the maximum amount to her company's employer-sponsored retirement plan as well as to a Roth IRA. And she has selected a retirement plan that will enable her to access her funds before retirement.

Cara established this plan of action more than three years ago with little or no investment experience. Her portfolio now consists of aggressive mutual funds invested in the high-tech industry, individual stocks that she researched and purchased through a stockbroker, and money market mutual funds that she uses to fund her frequent short trips to concerts and vacation hot spots. Her investment portfolio is growing in value, and she continues to look for other investment opportunities.

Cara's path to her dream is simple. First, she spends less than she earns. Second, she has made her wealth-building process automatic. Third, she regularly explores new investment options. And fourth, she intentionally increases her financial knowledge through reading, classes, conversation, and the Internet.

Chapter 3

The Confident Investor

The Bottom Line

Confidence comes with knowledge and experience. The distance between the confidence you have now and the confidence you seek is not far.

Cara's confidence came through experience, one step at a time. Today, she can say with confidence she can ...

- ❖ Retire at 45.
- ❖ Control her money instead of letting her money control her.
- ❖ Provide for her future by herself.
- ❖ Learn what she needs to know.
- ❖ Make choices that move her toward her goal.

How the Confident Investor Thinks

I remember the first time that I presented a seminar. I froze in front of the audience and stumbled my way through the unpleasant experience. When it was over, I vowed to never let that happen again, and it didn't. I learned what I needed to know to become a confident speaker.

Today, I think differently than I did then. I know that I can present information in a way that people can receive. I know that I can manage an audience and field questions. I know that I can operate the tools of speaking, such as microphones and PowerPoint presentations. Knowledge and experience have transformed the way I think about speaking.

The same can be said of Cara and every other person who invests. Their thinking has changed over time, and they see money, spending, opportunities, and their future in a particular way.

Successful investors think differently than noninvestors. They view money uniquely and develop patterns of behavior and thought that keep them in front financially. I want you to see how a confident investor thinks so that you can compare it to your own way of thinking and make any adjustments that you want.

About Money

Confident investors like Cara generally think differently about money than noninvestors. They think of money as a tool to help them achieve what they want. Like a key, money is a tool that can be used to unlock doors, important doors that determine the way a person lives today and in the future. In Cara's case, money is the tool that will fund her dream of retiring at 45 to a life of travel and other pursuits.

When confident investors look at their money, they generally ask themselves, "What's the best use of this money?" They weigh the answer carefully. They understand that every decision has consequences, and they look ahead to see what those consequences might be. Cara's choices about money are driven by her goal of early retirement. She knows, as investors do, that once the money is spent on, say, a blouse, it's gone. They can't use it anymore. They aren't opposed to buying blouses, but they are opposed to buying blouses thought-lessly. They know that the money for one blouse could be invested and grow to become enough to buy ten blouses in a few years.

Confident investors also ask themselves, "How can I make this money make more money?" They're experts at putting their money to work—employing it, so to speak, to create more. When money makes money, goals are achieved. That's how confident investors think about money.

I also notice that confident investors associate money with freedom. Money buys choices in one's life. As Idaho State Treasurer Ron Crane said at Boise's Everywoman's Money™ Conference, "Too often a lack of money keeps women in bondage to a life they don't want." Investors like the freedom that money gives them, and they keep their money making more money so that they can maintain that freedom.

How does this compare to the way you think about money? If you think about money like a confident investor, you will see it as the tool that can create the life you want.

Coaching Tip

If you work, you trade time for money. When you have enough money working for you, you can quit. You have a choice about whether you trade time for money. That is financial freedom.

About Spending

Confident investors prefer to spend their money on making more money before they spend it on things that won't make them money. Cara is funding her dream, so her first money each month is spent investing in that dream. She has a plan and sticks to it. She pays herself first, and then she pays her bills. She enjoys spending what's left on her life right now.

For investors, their goal drives their spending. They look at a pair of $80 shoes and know that it could buy two shares of a utility stock they've been watching. They may buy the shoes, but it's a careful choice, not a thoughtless one. For example, Cara could buy a new car. She loves new cars. But she doesn't drive one. It would cut into money that she is spending on her future, and she thinks that the trade-off is worth it.

Confident investors resist instant gratification, and you won't hear many of them rationalizing about why they just *had* to buy that new sofa. They are independent in their thinking about money and aren't swayed by what others do or buy.

For confident investors, spending is intentional and always in line with their plan. For them, this is the way to be sure that they will retain tomorrow the same life and freedom of choice that they enjoy today.

How does this compare with the way you think about spending? If you think about spending like a confident investor, you will see it as something that you do to support, not sabotage, your life plan.

About Opportunities

Confident investors are continually confronted with opportunities. The confident investors I know have a pattern of behaviors that help them filter opportunities:

1. They resist invading their existing investments (or their savings) at all costs. If seizing an opportunity means taking money from another investment, they probably won't do it. For example, if Cara owns stock in Microsoft and she wants to buy stock in Intel, she won't sell her Microsoft stock to get it. She wants both, so she will save to buy Intel.

2. They do their homework before deciding whether to pursue an investment opportunity. They research all aspects of the company until they feel confident that it will be a good investment.

3. They are decisive, and once they make a decision, they stick with it and don't look back.

4. They think about long-term security, not short-term volatility.

5. They learn from their mistakes and move on rather than vow to never invest again.

6. They know that opportunities come and go; if they don't catch this one, another will come along. They are patient.

7. They are skeptical and tend to go the other way when everyone else is investing in a trendy stock.

How does this compare with your thinking about opportunities? If you think about opportunities like a confident investor, you will see them as choices that are good for you only if they fit your timetable, risk level, and current financial situation.

About Companies

Confident investors see businesses as potential investments, not simply places to shop. They pay attention to a company's products, management changes, and signs of expansion.

They also understand balance sheets and can read the financials of a company. They know how to research using the opinions of analysts or research companies. This information is accessible over the Internet and at your local library.

Women are particularly good at spotting companies that might make good investments, because they are the world's chief consumers. They know what works and what doesn't work. They know what stores offer the best products and service. They know when a product that every mother wants hits the market, and they can tell you the same about what kids want. This puts women at an advantage in selecting companies to invest in.

Selecting individual stocks is time-consuming, so most investors have a few individual stock picks and let their stockbroker or financial planner make the rest.

How does this compare with your thinking about companies? If you think about companies like a confident investor, you will see them as potential money-makers for you.

Coaching Tip

Peter Lynch, the former portfolio manager of Fidelity Magellan Fund, suggests that you buy what you know. One of his best stock investments was the Sara Lee corporation, and he purchased the stock because his wife saw women buying pantyhose that were packaged in egg-shaped containers. This is why women are good investors. They can spot a trend happening.

About Choices

Confident investors see choices as trade-offs. They understand the risk/reward pyramid and do what they can to minimize risk while maximizing reward.

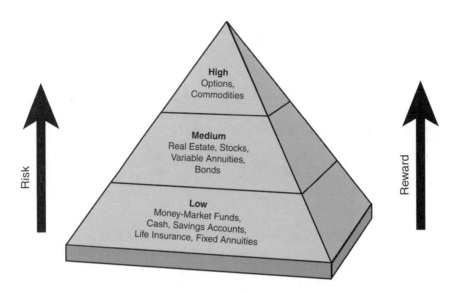

The risk/reward pyramid.

Investors always weigh possible outcomes, don't take risks lightly, and have little sense of urgency. They take time on the front end of a choice to save time and money on the back end.

Confident investors know that when they lose money, they have to make more money to replace it. They try to avoid this unpleasant experience.

How does this compare with your thinking about choices? If you think about choices like a confident investor, you will see them as financial moves that can help you or hurt you. You will also understand that for every choice you make, there is a trade-off.

About Risk

Confident investors do what they can to minimize risk. They don't want to lose money because it takes them in the wrong direction.

Reducing risk as an investor means that you will take these steps:

1. Invest in a number of different investment products. That way, if one drops, the others will make up for it. This is called asset allocation. You allocate your assets here and there across the investment spectrum.

2. Seek advice from a professional whom you trust and who knows you.

3. Continue learning so that you can spot bad advice when you hear it.

4. Stay true to your instincts.

5. Remember, risk exists whether you put your money in the bank, in the stock market, or under the mattress.

Having said that, I want you to know that confident investors expect to lose money, no matter how hard they try to avoid it. They've learned that not all stocks or funds will perform well, even when it appeared that they would. Loss is inevitable, but the success of the market over time supports investing.

Historic Range of Annual Returns 1985-1999

	Capital Preservation	Income	High Yield	Growth and Income	Growth	International	Aggressive Growth
Highest Annual Returns	8.9	21.27	37.23	31.45	37.55	47.98	41.65
Lowest Annual Returns	2.63	-3.53	-9.9	-4.45	-3.99	-11.05	-8.9
Average:	5.58%	8.12%	9.98%	15.56%	17.47%	15.69%	16.96%

The historic growth of stocks over time.

I've seen some investors lose money and never return to the market. Unfortunately, they've let their fear keep them from recovering and moving forward.

How does this compare with your thinking about risk? If you think about risk like a confident investor, you will take precautions, understand that some loss is inevitable, and stick with it anyway.

Coaching Tip

Don't mistake volatility for risk. Volatility is the ups and downs of the market.

About the Future

Like other confident investors, Cara is optimistic about her future. She doesn't worry about it because she has it covered financially. This allows her to spend joyfully today because she has set aside enough for tomorrow.

A sense of control over your future enables you to be flexible about it. For example, Cara might decide that she doesn't want to retire at 45 after all. But if she does retire, she'll have enough money in place to fund it.

This speaks to the importance of revisiting your goals once a year to be certain that you still want to do what you planned. Many things happen on the way to your future, and you want to be able to move in new directions if they are a closer fit to the person you have become.

The confident investor knows that goals are really just answers to the question of how she wants her life to be and that the important thing is to have enough money to support her choices.

How does this compare with your thinking about the future? If you think about the future like a confident investor, you will be optimistic and flexible because you will already have visited the future and deposited money in it.

Who the Confident Investor Trusts

The confident investor trusts herself first. She develops an instinct about investing and uses it in selecting investment products and advisors.

 Coaching Tip

Money is not security. Security comes from within. When you know you can take care of yourself, you have security.

In addition to trusting herself, to help her succeed financially, the confident investor assembles others to ...

Give Her Advice

Cara, like most investors, gets her advice from professionals and avoids advice from well-meaning family and friends.

Make Her Trades

She executes trades through a broker and occasionally on her own. Women increasingly are using online brokerage services and research tools, but most do this in addition to their work with a broker, not as a replacement.

Manage Her Earnings/Losses

The confident investor uses a tax professional but keeps accurate and organized records herself.

Create Her Financial Plan

She uses a financial planner as her financial quarterback to help oversee her entire financial condition and progress. She is very particular about who this person is and doesn't hesitate to interview several planners before settling on one in particular.

Build Her Estate

The confident investor relies on an estate-planning team, including her financial planner and an estate-planning attorney.

Monitor Her Progress

She reviews her own progress monthly and at least annually with advisers.

Protect Her Assets

The confident investor protects her assets by having her attorney draw up her will and trust.

Prepare Her Reports

More and more investors use computer software to track their money and print out reports other than those prepared by accountants and attorneys.

How the Confident Investor Learns

The successful investor is a learner. She reads, watches, talks, and takes classes. She creates her own reservoir of information, from subscribing to newspapers such as *The Wall Street Journal* or *The New York Times* to making financial sites such as financialmuse.com her Internet home page. She has her favorite financial channel on TV, such as CNBC, and tunes in to her favorite show, such as public television's Louis Rukeyser. As the investor's knowledge grows, so does her ability to screen information that comes to her from advisers and her skill in making smart decisions.

The confident investor knows that financial information is not beyond her ability to understand. She holds her advisers accountable and doesn't pretend that she understands something when she doesn't. She learns that if a professional can't describe a financial concept or product clearly, she may not want to continue the relationship.

The confident investor also likes to stay in step with technology. She may receive stock quotes and portfolio updates on her wireless phone or personal assistant.

She attends classes and seminars in her area and beyond. As she advances in her knowledge and activity, she may also choose to attend stockholders' meetings in various parts of the country.

The confident investor knows that learning is an essential ingredient to ongoing success. Most enjoy it and find it satisfying to stay on the cutting edge of information about the resources that will fund their future.

How does this compare with the way you think about learning? If you think like a confident investor, you will see learning as your responsibility to yourself and an activity that will increase your future prosperity.

Olivia Mellan

Money Therapy

Once women start learning about investing and doing it, they actually make better, more consistent and rational decisions than many men, who are often swayed by tips from friends (that "hot stock" of the week) and by a desire to outperform their friends. So take heart—remember that women's investment clubs have outperformed men's clubs for most of the years since women have been flocking to join them. Go, women!

What the Confident Investor Does

Let's see what the confident investor does …

With Her Earnings

She pays herself first, invests at least 10 percent of her income (often more), participates in employer-sponsored plans, and uses advisers to help her make smart choices about her earnings.

To Manage Advisers

She schedules appointments as needed with her advisers, and she never misses her annual appointments with them.

To Fit Investing into Her Busy Life

She utilizes automatic investment programs deducted from her payroll and savings accounts, lets a stock information service send her data over the Internet or her wireless device, reads the financial column over coffee in the morning, and meets with other women on the same financial path once a week over lunch.

To Manage Her Fears

The confident investor …

1. Conveys her concerns to her advisers immediately.
2. Faces her fears instead of letting them fester.
3. Leaves little or no room for wondering how things are by looking at all statements monthly.
4. Listens to sources that are sound, not sensational. For example, when the market goes down a few points, many television reporters say, "The market took a tumble today." But when it goes up a few points, they report "a modest gain."

The Bottom Line

Gaining confidence as an investor will produce rewards beyond the financial. It will increase your sense of control over yourself and your future, giving you a financial peace of mind that noninvestors can't experience.

Reader's Journal:

Knowledge Gained:

_____

_____

_____

_____

_____

_____

_____

_____

_____

_____

Steps I Will Take:

_____

_____

_____

_____

_____

_____

_____

_____

_____

_____

Melissa, a beautiful woman in her late 40s, entered my seminar for beginning investors, disguising her panic with cool confidence. During the class, she took detailed notes, and by her questions about investing for retirement, I knew what she was there to learn.

She scheduled an appointment with me after the seminar. In it, I learned just how serious her situation was. Melissa had worked for the Internal Revenue Service for more than 20 years and had not saved a dime for retirement. Her pension would not support her lifestyle. She spent most of her money on clothing, travel, and cars. She didn't own a home and had never been married. Her boyfriend had no desire to get married, although she hung on in hopes that he would change his mind.

I asked Melissa what her goals were. She said, "Debbie, I have worked to earn money all my life, and now it's time for me to make my money work when I am no longer able to."

Good answer. That is the purpose of investing.

Chapter 4

What Is Investing?

The Bottom Line

Investing is putting your money in a place where it can earn more money on its own, while you sleep, eat, or hop a ship to Madrid. The most common and profitable place to invest is in stocks of companies.

Recently, I accompanied my friend Twila to the sporting goods store while she bought a canoe, something that she had dreamed of having since she was a child. From the front of the store, we could see the canoes displayed about 15 aisles back. The closer we got, the more difficult the mission seemed to be. Out of so many canoes, how would we choose the right one for Twila?

The answer became clear as the salesman asked Twila some simple questions. How many people will be riding in the canoe? *Up to three people.* How long do you want the canoe to last? *She wanted it to become a canoe that could be passed down to her nieces and nephews.* How much money do you want to spend? *Under $500.* With each of Twila's answers, canoes were eliminated until we were standing in front of two canoes that fit her needs, a green one and a red one. Twila likes red, so that's the canoe she bought.

The same process of elimination simplifies your investment choices, which at first can seem confusing. The key questions are ...

1. Do you want your money to grow over time, produce immediate income, or both?

2. How much time do you have for your money to work?

Melissa wanted her money to grow over time to produce money to live on once she stopped working. She had about 15 years before she needed that income to begin. These answers sent her to the financial marketplace, known as the stock exchange, to acquire the financial products she needed. It didn't take her long to find her way around.

The Stock Exchanges

Financial assets such as stocks and bonds are exchanged, or traded, in the financial marketplace. Stocks and bonds both trade on the stock exchanges. There are several exchanges in the financial marketplace, including ...

❖ The New York Stock Exchange (NYSE).

❖ The American Stock Exchange (ASE).

❖ The Pacific Stock Exchange (PSE).

The New York Stock Exchange would be considered a high-end retailer, like Saks Fifth Avenue, because most of the companies in it are larger and meet stiff requirements to be listed there. On the other hand, many other companies trade on the NASDAQ stock market and over-the-counter markets. These markets are different in that they are not floor-based exchanges. In the NASDAQ stock market, stocks and bonds are traded electronically and buyers and sellers are matched by sophisticated computer networks. over-the-counter markets are where stocks that are not listed on an exchange are traded.

Companies raise money by issuing one of two things: debt securities, also known as bonds, or equity securities, also known as stocks.

Investing is exchanging money for a stock or a bond that either grows your money or gives you immediate income. If you buy stock, you're buying a share, or equity, in a company. As that company stock increases in value, so does the value of your investment. In other words, the $25 that you paid for a share of ownership in Pepsi that is now worth $50 has doubled your money. Your money has grown. It has worked for you without you having to work for it.

If you buy a bond, you're lending money to a company, city, or organization to complete a project such as the building of a new City Hall. In return, the organization returns all of your money at a stated time in the future and in the meantime pays you interest, or income, for loaning the money.

Like Melissa, the confident investor makes some decisions:

1. Identifies what she needs her money to do: grow, produce income, or both
2. Estimates the time available to do it
3. Determines the best financial product(s) for achieving her goal(s): stocks, bonds, or both

The Debt, or Bond, Market

The debt, or bond, market is where governments and corporations needing to borrow money are matched with investors who have money to lend. Investors in the debt market want income from the money they lend.

Here's how the debt market works. If a company or local government needs money to buy equipment or build a new facility and doesn't want to take out a bank loan for one reason or another, the company or government may choose to issue bonds to sell to investors like you.

Bonds would be issued by the company and an investment banker would be hired. The investment banker takes on the risk of finding investors to buy the bonds. If the banker needs help finding investors, he may create a "syndicate" of other brokers to help him sell the bonds. The members of the syndicate, usually investment companies and securities firms, earn a fee or commission based on what they sell to their customers.

Members of the syndicate act as middlemen, buying from those issuing the bonds and selling to investors in what is called the *primary market.*

When the bonds have been issued, bond dealers use their capital to maintain active *secondary markets,* bidding for bonds that investors want to sell and offering bonds from their inventory to investors who want to buy.

The bond market functions largely as an "over-the-counter" market. This is an electronic market where securities are bought and sold from dealer to dealer, who in turn buy from and sell to investors. Unlike the stock exchanges where there are traders on the floor buying and selling, most of these transactions are done over computers and phones.

Total Market Value Outstanding*

Stocks	$8.9 trillion
Bonds	$11.1 trillion

*According to the Bond Market Association as of 1996

The bond market versus the stock market.

Although bonds are debt obligations, they do carry risk. The risk is the issuing company's ability to pay back the investors. Corporations and governments are rated based on their financial stability and ability to return the principal to investors. The rating affects the interest rate that you earn on your loan, as well as the confidence that you have in getting your principal back.

Many of us as kids had our own savings, or passbook, accounts. Every week or so, we made a deposit by filling out a deposit slip and handing it to the teller with our little blue or black book. The teller made an entry in the book and stamped it with a deposit verification. We kept track of the balance as it grew, and every three months or so we received a statement from the bank detailing how many deposits we made and how much interest we had earned. The interest was reported as interest income. Interest income is one form of earning money on your money.

As our money grew, so did the amount of interest we earned. More money, more interest. If we had $500, we could purchase a certificate of deposit (CD) by locking our money up for six months or a year and then earn even more interest, or income, on it.

One of the first bonds that most of us encounter is a savings bond. Savings bonds don't pay interest in the strictest sense of the word. Instead, you buy them at a discount and then their value increases over time, until they mature and are worth the amount imprinted on the face of the bonds.

The United States government is one of the biggest issuers of bonds. It issues Treasury bills, notes, and bonds that mature anywhere from 6 months to 30 years down the road. All of these bonds pay interest, or income. You loan your money to the government, and the government pays you for the use of your money.

Although bonds pay an income, historically they have not kept up with or significantly outpaced inflation. Still, they have an important place in the investing equation (see Chapter 9, "How to Invest in Bonds," to find out why).

If Melissa had needed immediate income rather than long-term growth, she would have invested in bonds. Her income would be the interest that she was paid on the money that she loaned.

There are many types of bonds. The type of bond that you purchase will depend upon when you need the money back and how much interest, or income, you want to earn.

Learn how to invest in bonds in Chapter 9.

The Equity, or Stock, Market

One of the other ways to invest is for growth. This means that you want your money to grow over time. The most common form of growth investing is stocks or stock mutual funds. When you invest in stocks, you purchase a share of a company in hopes that the company—and, therefore, its shares—will increase in value.

I think that women have an advantage when it comes to investing for growth because we come face to face with the products that these companies produce. We know Procter and Gamble, Kellogg's, and Coca-Cola. In fact, women influence more than 70 percent of all the buying decisions of households in the country. Now that more and more women are investing, we will be not only consumers, but also owners of the products we buy.

For as long as I can remember, my mother has used only Tide detergent for washing clothes. I, on the other hand, usually buy what's on sale. On her visits to my home, she says, "Why do you bother buying this cheap detergent? You end up using twice as much to get the same results as the more expensive one." My mother is not alone in her sentiment. Millions of other women feel the same way, making Procter and Gamble (the company that makes Tide) a profitable investment over the years. I often wonder how different my mother's life would be now if she had actually taken her observations one step further and bought shares in Procter and Gamble.

I'm not recommending that you buy shares in Procter and Gamble, but let's take a look at why it might have been a good investment for my mother. The company went public in 1890. Over the years, it has developed more than 300 brands, including Tampax, Pringles, Folger's coffee, Dawn, and Bounty. Procter and Gamble knows how to make successful products, and its rise in value as a company proves it.

Once a company "goes public," or sells shares of ownership to investors, it uses some of the money from the proceeds of the sale to expand and fund its growth. When it becomes consistently profitable, it distributes those profits to shareholders as dividends. When you receive a dividend, you can decide to spend the money or to tell the company to use the dividend to buy more shares of stock. This is called "dividend reinvestment" and is the way many investors accumulate large numbers of shares of a company without ever investing more of their own money in it.

If my mother had invested $1,000 in shares of Procter and Gamble 20 years ago and had reinvested her dividends, that investment would be worth $261,340 today. She would have some exciting choices. She could cash in her dividends and use them to supplement her Social Security payments, or she could sell just enough shares to get a lump sum to buy a car or pay for a vacation. Her investment would now be providing the income that she needs at retirement. That is the point of investing.

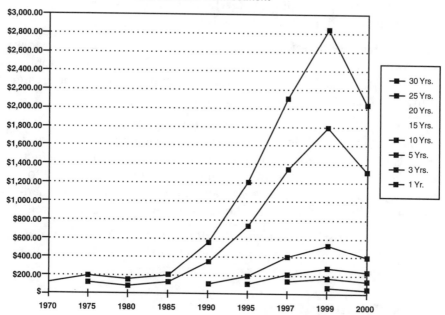

Dividend reinvestment chart on Procter and Gamble.

Study the accompanying chart to see the effect that investing and reinvesting dividends can have on your bottom line. Notice that in the early years, the shares accumulate slowly and the price of the shares fluctuates. As time passes and the number of shares increases, the amount of the dividend increases as well, buying even more shares. This combination of results is called "dollar cost averaging," or buying shares at different prices, and "compound growth." In fact, when the share price decreases in value, you're able to purchase more shares with the dividends, as if it were on sale. Now, imagine the wealth that you would build on top of this if you were also adding $25 or $50 to your investment every month.

This is how wealth is built through equity investing. This is the type of growth that Melissa was after.

When companies issue stock and offer shares to the public, they become public companies that trade shares on the stock exchange. As with a bond offering, an investment banker is hired to find investors and often forms a syndicate of brokers to help.

Companies issuing stock, or shares, sell to investors like Melissa who want to profit from a company's performance. When a company's profits increase, so does its value. When a company's value goes up, so does its stock, and investors make money.

The risk of equity investing, of course, is that a company whose stock you own may not be profitable or may not be able to sustain profitability. This underlines the importance of choosing your stocks carefully, which is not difficult with wise and experienced help.

You've seen the value of companies go up and down, depending on public sentiment, politics, who is joining or leaving a company, and what is in the wind about a new product in development. This fluctuation adds to the challenge of investing, especially if you choose to buy and manage your stocks personally rather than have them managed professionally. But women do it every day, and they do it well.

Even with the risk, stocks have outperformed other investment tools such as bonds and real estate over time, making investing in stocks the most reliable way to grow your money long term.

Investing for Income

If you determine that you need income, you must decide what type of bond will produce the income and level of risk you require. The shortest way to that information is by answering questions like these:

1. Why do I need income? Is it to supplement my current earnings? Is it to pay for a specific expense such as a car note, a mortgage, or another obligation?

2. How often do I need to receive the income? Monthly, semiannually, annually?

3. Would I prefer the income to be taxable or tax-free? (No, that question isn't as obvious as it seems.) The different types of bonds and their features are covered in Chapter 9.

4. What rate of return (the amount you earn on an investment) am I trying to achieve?

5. Do I need a guarantee of my principal, or am I willing to take on more risk for more return?

Your answers will determine the type of bond you need.

Esther is recently retired and considering a Treasury bond to supplement her Social Security and pension income. She can wait for payment every six months, and she wants her principal to be guaranteed.

On a bond that matures in 10 years, meaning that in 10 years she will get all of her money back, Esther would receive 6 percent interest. She is concerned that in 10 years, interest rates might increase and she would miss the chance to earn higher interest because her rate of return would be locked in.

Let's look at Esther's needs and concerns and decide whether a Treasury bond is the best investment tool for her.

- ❖ Esther needs income, so a bond is the appropriate investment product for her.
- ❖ She can wait for payment every six months, which fits the Treasury bond payment schedule.
- ❖ Her interest payments will be taxable, but because she needs the income as a supplement to her Social Security and pension, taxes probably aren't a big concern.
- ❖ She wants her investment guaranteed, and a Treasury bond is about the safest income investment available.
- ❖ Although there is a good chance that interest rates will increase over 10 years and she may miss out on higher returns, she is willing to invest in a bond to guarantee the income she needs.

Esther has made the best decision for her situation.

Investing for Growth

Melissa's income is adequate, but she is playing catch-up on retirement savings. She must invest for growth. In other words, she must invest in equity, or stocks.

Just as there is a variety of bonds and levels of risk, there is a variety of stocks and levels of risk. To help Melissa select the best stocks for her goals, I asked her these questions:

1. How much can you afford to invest for the long term?
2. What type of companies do you want to invest in?
3. Do you want to research companies on your own or have someone help you?

4. How much risk are you willing to take to achieve your goals?

5. Do you want to invest moderately or aggressively?

6. How much time do you want to invest in investing?

Imagine

What is investing? It is taking responsibility for your financial life in a way that gives you the greatest possible chance of earning the money that you need to live the life you've planned. Investing well will do that for you with the least amount of effort because your money will earn money while you're sleeping.

Let me show you what I mean by imagining that you got in on the first issue of Wal-Mart stock. Let's say that when Wal-Mart came to your town, you noticed that the stores were big, the staff was friendly, and the prices were low. You instructed your stockbroker to buy you 100 shares. In 1970, Wal-Mart offered 300,000 shares to the public for $16.50 each. You would have paid $1,650 for your 100 shares.

With the money raised from selling those shares, Wal-Mart built more stores across the United States. As Wal-Mart increased its profitability, it distributed dividends to its investors. Most of those investors re-invested the dividends into more shares. If you had done that, you would now have more than 204,800 shares of Wal-Mart stock, at a value of $9,446,400.

The only type of investment that gives you the opportunity to earn a return of this type is stock. Not all companies perform as well as Wal-Mart, but most people would be happy to find one that performs half that well—and many do.

There are women around you who consistently invest in the stock market. Like Melissa, they are enjoying a quiet confidence that only investors know.

Investing vs. Saving

How do you know whether to save or invest? This is an important question, and the answer is quite simple.

Saving

Setting money aside for urgent needs and opportunities is a classic habit of confident investors. There are things we need or want that require us to hold our money and wait.

Karen McCall, author of *It's Your Money,* tells the story of her daughter who, like many of us, battled the urge to spend instead of save. Karen had modeled spending instead of saving, suffered dramatic consequences, and worked her way out of it. In the process, her grown children took notice and began following the new pattern that she was setting.

Karen's daughter began saving. One day Karen got a call. Her daughter said, "Mom, do you want the bad news or the good news?"

Karen said, "I want both." Her daughter said, "Well, the bad news is that I dented my car. The good news is that I had the money to pay for it!" In talking to Karen later, her daughter said that having the money to pay for the damage brought her so much joy that the damage to the car didn't seem like a big deal.

As Karen says, having a savings account makes a dented car a normal life event, not a reason for chaos and panic.

Inevitably, the washer breaks down. The kids grow out of shoes. The wind blows the fence into the neighbor's yard. A pipe under the house breaks.

Or, your friends are going skiing for the weekend and you want to go, too. Your favorite singer is performing two states away. You hear about a company that's about to go public, and you want to buy stock.

Savings accounts permit you to respond quickly without having to dip into credit, borrow the money from someone else, or miss out on opportunities. Although I believe that credit cards are convenient and useful for people who know how to manage their credit, I know from personal experience and from observing others that they can become a substitute for savings. A $500 repair becomes a long-term credit card debt with monthly payments.

Cara, from Chapter 3, "The Confident Investor," is an experienced saver. She saved for vacations but didn't invest. Ida, from Chapter 2, "Here You Are," also saved. She didn't want to risk losing her cash. They both came to the realization that their money could be put to work more effectively. They invested a great deal of it and kept the rest in savings.

How did Cara and Ida know how much to keep in their savings accounts? The same way you will know—by answering a simple question: When do you want your money back?

Cara knew that she was going to Brazil in 14 months, so she put that money in a savings account. Ida plans to buy a car in two years, so she has put money for a down payment aside rather than invest it.

The basic timetable for deciding whether to save or invest is five years. If you want your money back within five years, save it. If you want it back beyond five years, invest it. Of course, sometimes you might invest money even if you want it back within five years, but this is a general recommendation.

Confident investors get into the savings habit. They like knowing that there is money set aside for urgent needs and opportunities. Ideally, they have six months of expenses set aside in savings.

There are a number of interest-bearing savings tools.

Description	Institution
1. Certificates of Deposits	Bank
2. Money Market Accounts	Bank
3. Money Market Mutual Funds	Investment Company
4. Treasury Bills, Notes	Government

Investing

The shift that both Cara and Ida made after they understood the difference between saving and investing has produced earnings that they would not have had if they had remained only savers.

In Cara's case, we set aside enough savings to meet her needs. Then we earmarked a significant portion of her earnings for long-term investment. She maximized her 401(k) contribution to reduce her tax liabilities because she was single. Plus, the investment would grow without being taxed every year. Cara also chose to open an individual retirement account (IRA). She decided to invest at least 20 percent of her income toward her early retirement goal. She also wanted to buy a house in a few years and needed to grow the down payment. Cara's total investment strategy was pretty clear: Buy a house and save for early retirement. With that kind of clarity and determination, she was on her way.

Saving and Investing: Confusing the Two Can Be Costly

Cara and I talked weekly once her plan was in place, and she was doing well. Then several weeks passed and I didn't hear from her. I assumed that her learning curve had hit a plateau, which is why she hadn't called. I was wrong. Instead, Cara was learning a hard lesson and didn't want to tell me about her misfortune.

Like most investors, Cara keeps an eye open for emerging investment opportunities. She knew that UPS was going public, and she instructed her broker to buy shares on opening day using money from her savings account. She had been saving that money for a down payment on the home that she planned to buy in two years. She believed that the stock would do what others typically did—increase rapidly after opening. The stock of UPS more than doubled as she had assumed but because she did not receive shares of the initial public offering she instructed her broker to buy at the market opening. She purchased UPS stock at the highest price of the day and it still has not reached the price she paid. Cara is optimistic that the stock will rise in value, but the temporary loss of her savings forced her to make other choices about the down payment on her house.

Cara had confused saving with investing, and it cost her both time and money, a lesson that she will not forget.

The confident investor understands these points:

1. You save your money for short-term needs of five years or less.
2. You invest your money for long-term needs of five years or more.
3. Reinvesting dividends is a way to increase the number of shares that you own without spending extra to buy them.
4. When compounding kicks in, wealth builds quickly. (See Chapter 5, "Reasons for Investing," for more on compounding.)

The Bottom Line

If you invest wisely, you're giving your money its best chance at making more money. This means that investing well gives you the best chance at living out your life plan.

Reader's Journal:

Knowledge Gained:

_____

_____

_____

_____

_____

_____

_____

_____

_____

_____

Steps I Will Take:

_____

_____

_____

_____

_____

_____

_____

_____

_____

_____

Julia was a wild success at her job as an account executive for a prestigious ad agency. She enjoyed her paycheck every month—all of it and more. Her credit card debt was mounting, and she figured that she could always get another one when those were maxed out. She paid her bills on time, which made her feel on top of her finances. She didn't notice that there was less and less cash to spend every month because it was being sucked up by credit card payments.

One day, Julia's friends, Amy and Mike, announced that they were moving to Ohio and were going to sell their house. They knew that Julia loved their house, and they offered it to her before putting it on the market. Julia was excited and told them that she would buy it. But when she went to the lender for a home loan, she was turned down. She didn't have enough cash, and her credit card debt was too high. Julia was crushed and embarrassed. That's when a friend referred her to me.

Julia had to face the truth, and it turned her money life around. Today she is an investor and a saver. Her debt is diminishing, and she uses her credit cards only for convenience, paying the balance monthly. She still enjoys great clothes and travel, but she has learned to control her choices. Best of all, Julia will be ready when her next opportunity knocks.

Karen married during college and soon afterward gave birth to Jenna. She stayed home with Jenna while her husband launched and advanced his career. Karen was the perfect suburban mom. Her house was immaculate, and she was a leader in the PTA, in Girl Scouts, and, as Jenna grew older, in community events and volunteering. Her husband, by now a successful corporate executive, joked that it didn't make sense for her to work because they would only have to pay more taxes.

One day her husband announced he was moving to California—without her and Jenna. Karen was devastated. She had no savings of her own and hadn't worked since college. In the divorce settlement, Karen had received half of her husband's 401(k). She was using it for living expenses, including a mortgage on a house much too big and expensive for them, because she wanted to protect Jenna from a downsized life.

When she told me her story, I asked her if she realized that she was spending her future. She said, "I know. I can't help it. My daughter has been through enough." Several discussions later, Karen decided to make alternative choices that wouldn't jeopardize what little savings she had of her own.

Chapter 5

Reasons for Investing

The Bottom Line

Investing allows you to leverage the money that comes into your life so that you will have enough to meet the opportunities and responsibilities that life hands you.

Some challenges can be met only with money. Money in your pocket means confidently meeting those challenges. It means control over your choices. Karen's story is the rule more than the exception, and every day, women are thrown into chaos that could be resolved with financial independence. It has been said, "Riches do not produce happiness, but neither does poverty." Money is not the answer to all problems, but it does allow you to respond better to what life hands you. Teresa Wilhelmi, breast cancer survivor and a member of the Everywoman's Money™

Empowerment Team, says that her financial chaos not only worsened her fight with the disease, but it also competed with it as a personal struggle. Her comment reveals how deeply money problems affect us.

Karen had left college, got married, and had a child. She was out of the workforce for 15 years and returned with limited work experience and no college degree. She had never even thought about investing for herself. The reality is that women are out of the workforce an average of 11½ years, according to the U.S. Census Bureau. This results in smaller pensions and retirement checks, a gap that must be filled. The way to overcome this gap is to invest for your future regardless of the status of your employment.

Here's why all of us need to start an investment plan as soon as possible:

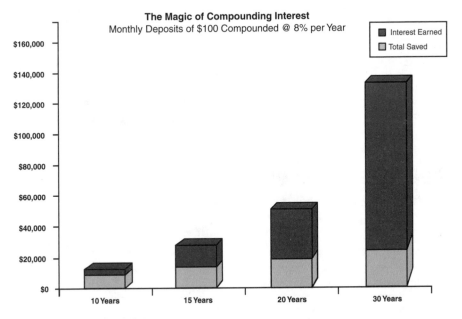

The power of compounding.

Invest to Create Wealth

Investing enables you to create wealth—money above and beyond what you earn.

Wealth is simply accumulating assets—in this case, money. Your level of wealth will depend on how much you can and want to build.

Investing is the fastest way to create the wealth you need to live the life that you plan—and to act on opportunities such as Julia's chance to buy her friends' house. The "Magic of Compounding Interest" figure proves this point. In this case, the investment was in the stock market. Compounding is the secret ingredient that savings tools don't have. It's what makes your money make more money so that you don't have to. While it's never too late to invest, the earlier you begin, the more assets you will have in the future.

The women we have featured as "everywomen" in this book share a common theme: They were afraid of risk. Being risk-averse is typical of women and is part of the reason we have stayed away from investing. We don't want to lose what we've saved and earned. Although there are no guarantees that your investments will always make money, history proves that over time they do.

Cara and Ida were both excellent money managers and savers. Yet a significant percentage of their savings was bringing very low returns, sometimes so low that they were actually losing money without knowing it (because of inflation). Now, *that's* risk. The less return on your money you get, the longer it takes for that money to grow. The opposite, of course, is also true. The more return on your money you get, the faster it grows. Confident investors know where their line of comfort is on the risk/return scale. If you're new at investing, you'll learn what your tolerance is as well.

The Rule of 72

One of the simplest and most useful tools that you can use to determine how long it will take your money to grow is the "Rule of 72." You simply divide the rate of return that you're earning on your investments into the number 72. The answer reveals how long it will take your money to double in value.

The following figure compares a 29-year-old's $10,000 investment in a money market, a bond, and stocks. As the second column shows, $10,000 invested in a money market at 4 percent doubles in 12 years. The same money invested in stocks at 12 percent doubles every six years. As your money grows, you have a larger amount to double. The Rule of 72 will help you determine how long it will take you to reach a goal. Although your money will eventually double in any of these financial products, it has the best chance to grow more rapidly when you invest it in stock.

Age	4% Money Market	Age	6% Bond	Age	12% Stocks
29	10,000	29	10,000	29	10,000
47	20,000	41	20,000	35	20,000
65	40,000	53	40,000	41	40,000
		65	80,000	47	80,000
				53	160,000
				59	320,000
				65	640,000

The Rule of 72.

If you want to think about wealth like a confident investor, you will see wealth as simply the money you create to live the life that you plan, and you will see investing in stock as the preferred way to do it.

Invest to Provide for Your Loved Ones

Investing can make it easier for you to give good care to those you love.

When Karen's husband left, she had few options. She chose to proceed as usual, not wanting to disrupt her daughter's life. Although this is understandable, it endangered the two people she most needed to protect, her daughter and herself. She continued to pay the high mortgage on her home to shield her daughter from the reality that they were now living at a much lower standard.

When Karen became convinced that it was less important to keep up appearances than to risk serious financial decay, she chose to preserve the few assets that she had. They became the seed of the wealth she is building for her future. During the following year, she made some key decisions that paved her way to financial freedom:

1. She sold her house and moved into a two-bedroom condo.
2. She invested the proceeds from the sale in a money market mutual fund.

3. She completed a course for certification in software training, a continuation of the degree in computer science that she had been working on when she left college to marry.

4. Upon graduation, she landed a job in Florida.

Karen's wealth-building actions changed her course. She has invested her portion of her husband's retirement assets in a Rollover IRA. She also invested some of the money from the sale of her house in a mutual fund for Jenna's college tuition.

Investing for Jenna's education gave Karen a real sense of power. She had the power all along; investing helped her exercise it.

Coaching Tip

Don't use money in your IRA or 401(k) plan unless you absolutely have to. There is a penalty for withdrawing the money before age 59½. You are putting this money away for your old age. Letting it grow is a very good idea. Pretend you don't even have it.

Invest for a Raise

Investing lets you get a raise whether your boss gives you one or not. It also gives you a raise in spite of the bite of rising costs.

It wasn't hard to convince Karen to set aside funds for her daughter's education. All she had to do to understand was to see how her own tuition costs had increased since she was in college. The cost per credit hour was four times what she had paid 15 years earlier. That's the result of inflation, the rising cost of goods and services. As prices increase, the purchasing power of a dollar is reduced: higher prices, lower dollar power. For example, $10,000 in 1989 would buy only $7,300 today. (Visit www.nestegg.com/inflation to estimate what college might cost in 10 years. Use the inflation calculator at that site to calculate the purchasing power of your money over certain periods of time.)

Let's look at inflation from another perspective, the earnings perspective. If you feel like you're on a treadmill when it comes to earning money, inflation is the reason. If a dollar today doesn't buy what it did 10 years ago, then what you were earning back then won't carry you today. In other words, if you were earning $30,000 10 years ago, you would need to be earning $41,000 today to stay even. To have truly gotten a raise, you would need to be earning more than that.

What does inflation have to do with investing? Refer to our "Rule of 72" chart to find out. Deduct at least 3 percent from the Money Market column for inflation. Your return on bonds after inflation would be cut in half. Inflation is a silent enemy that threatens every dime you earn or spend. The only investment that has far outpaced inflation over time is stocks.

A confident investor fights inflation with investments.

Invest to Have Enough

Investing helps women fill the gap that they often face financially. You're the one living your life, so you're the one in charge of making sure that you have enough money to last your entire life. How will you do it?

It's true that women live longer than men, by an average of seven years. Seven years is a long time when you don't have enough. You want to have the money to take care of yourself. Without it, life is difficult—as many elderly women know.

Coaching Tip

It may be difficult to be old, but it's *really* difficult to be old and poor. Old women who are poor have a very hard time getting good medical care.

It takes courage to be responsible for yourself.

It's true, too, that many of us still earn less than men, meaning that we have to make less money go further. Plus, we leave the workforce to care for families, so we often don't qualify for pensions or we have less time to build up Social Security and retirement. Investing can help women meet such financial challenges confidently. Investing can help us create alternatives to being without, to missing out on pensions, and to earning less.

You may not qualify for a retirement plan from an employer, but you can create an alternative on your own. The investment vehicles are there to be deployed, even at the rate of $25 a month. Even small amounts invested systematically can really add up.

Wealth is not created in a few days. It is built over time. Look at what a small amount can do:

The key to investing is to keep it going consistently. You cannot afford to do nothing. If you didn't know it before reading this book, you know it now. To replace an income of $50,000, you need more than half a million saved to provide that income at retirement.

The only way to eat an elephant of that size is one bite at time.

Invest to Create an Estate

More and more women are leaving sizeable estates to the people and causes that they care about. For the most part, investing has enabled them to do it. Although your first priority is to make certain that you have enough to live on while you're alive, you may also be able to build assets that exceed your life needs and help support the lives and dreams of others.

Julia set a new standard of money sense among her friends. It's catching on, and her friends can be heard talking about stocks the way they talk about clothes. Lately, Julia has been captured by the idea that she could leave an estate for the education of her niece and nephews.

Karen was extremely pleased with the example that she set for her daughter. She believes that it will become a model that her daughter adapts to her own life, and she feels more confident about her daughter's financial future because of it. It frees her daughter to muster the courage to take on responsibility for her own financial success.

An estate is one way that your investments can continue to grow long after you are gone.

Olivia Mellan

Money Therapy

If you're still telling yourself, "Maybe other women can do this, but not me," why not take a few minutes to write down your self-doubting beliefs, and think of evidence to contradict them? Also, write down all your fears about money and investing. Once you've fleshed out the worst-case scenarios and what you'd do if, God forbid, they happened, you should be able to move on to formulate positive statements of what you can create with your money, if you just allot a little time and effort to it.

Invest to Make a Difference

Individual donors are responsible for 90 percent of the contributions made to charitable organizations. These people are using their money to make a difference. In many cases, investments have made it possible.

As you know, a side benefit to giving to charities is receiving a tax advantage. In a sense, the IRS encourages you to give. Just think of the many causes that benefit from charitable giving: the arts, public broadcasting, education, domestic violence prevention, youth services, medical assistance, economic development, and environmental protection. Which of these stir you? Which of them would you like to see prosper? Write it into your plan.

Money can bless, and investing can strengthen your ability to be on the giving end of that blessing.

The Bottom Line

Women who invest create the wealth necessary for financial freedom. This freedom enables them to live and give in satisfying ways.

Reader's Journal:

Knowledge Gained:

_____
_____
_____
_____
_____
_____
_____
_____
_____
_____

Steps I Will Take:

_____
_____
_____
_____
_____
_____
_____
_____
_____
_____

Laura, a friend of mine, has been a cosmetologist for more than 20 years. Regardless of how much money passed through her hands in wages, tips, and gifts, she never seemed to have enough left over to save, much less invest.

Although she had a retirement account through her employer, Laura realized that it would not be enough to replace her income when she stopped working. We discussed alternatives that would allow her to invest more. I suggested a few books that she could read and mutual funds that she could research to help address her needs.

Laura wanted to send her son to an exclusive boys' school. That meant spending an extra thousand dollars a month. How could she possibly invest for retirement, something that she had also become passionate about, and find the money to send her son to an expensive school? As Laura contemplated this issue, she was pressed to prioritize her life, to be sure she was using her money in the best way.

Laura knew that she made a significant amount of money in tips, but she didn't know how much it actually was and where it went every month. She came up with a solution: She would keep track of every dollar that came in and went out. She bought a small pink notebook to use as her money diary. This exercise was illuminating. Her notebook filled up with daily entries showing what she received and what she spent.

On her day off, Laura transferred the content of that week's notebook entries to a ledger. She then added them up to determine a weekly figure for each category. This "cash flow" analysis was life changing.

Laura discovered that she was earning several hundred dollars in tips each week. It became clear that if she adjusted her spending habits, she would indeed have enough to send her son to the exclusive school. Not only that, but she could also afford to fund her retirement plan every month.

Laura was motivated by her urge to furnish her son with an education that she believed would be best for him. She followed her own logic, which worked exactly as it should.

Laura was excited to show me what she had accomplished. I was amazed. I asked her if she had had to make any huge sacrifices and deprive herself of any luxuries that she was accustomed to. Laura said, "No, I don't feel deprived. I feel powerful. I finally have control over my money, which has left me with a feeling of peace and security."

Chapter 6

Finding the Money to Invest

The Bottom Line

You have, or can create, the money you need to invest.

One of the best things that you can immediately do for yourself is to start investing, or to increase the amount that you invest. How do you find or create the money? Good question. Let's find out.

You've got a lot going for you:

1. Investing has never been easier.
2. Investing has never required less money to get started.
3. There are simple ways to trim spending.

4. There are many ways to create income in addition to what you earn already.

5. The stakes and rewards have never been higher.

Where's Money?

Finding money within your existing money picture requires something of a "Where's Waldo?" search, but in this case, it's a "Where's Money?" search. You search your picture for green.

To do your "Where's Money?" search, you must be able to see the picture clearly. Laura couldn't pull her picture into view until she became an expert on what she earned and how she spent it. She was motivated to track her spending by her passionate desire for a good education for her son and an adequate retirement for herself.

If I had told Laura to track her spending before she was motivated, she wouldn't have done it. It would have been a chore instead of a mission. Watching what you spend is like watching what you eat. You do it because it's important to you, or you don't do it because it doesn't matter as much to you as you thought it did.

What is your motivation for finding money?

- ❖ I want to be a responsible money manager.
- ❖ I want to become an investor.
- ❖ I want to increase the amount I invest.
- ❖ I want to start my own business.
- ❖ I want to assemble my emergency savings nest egg.
- ❖ I want to invest in a particular company.
- ❖ I want to invest for my child's education.
- ❖ I want to invest for immediate income through bonds.
- ❖ I want to get my financial act together, and this is the first step.
- ❖ I want to save for a down payment on a home.
- ❖ I have a dream to _____.

How much of an expert are you at knowing what you earn and spend? Step onto Laura's path and follow her example.

Your Tracking Device

Laura chose a small pink notebook as her tracking device. What will you use to track your earning and spending?

- ❖ Notebook
- ❖ Mini cassette recorder
- ❖ Hand-held wireless, such as a Palm or Handspring device

Choose a tracking device that you can use instantly. Also use something that you either already have or can get today or tomorrow. Get at it now.

Your Spreadsheet

Laura recorded the week's earnings and spending onto a spreadsheet or ledger on her day off. What will your spreadsheet be?

- ❖ Paper spreadsheet from an office supply store
- ❖ Computerized spreadsheet already installed on your computer, such as Excel
- ❖ Software spreadsheet that you purchase, such as Quicken

Your Schedule

Next question: When will you enter your tracking data? Choose a time that you know you can keep so that you don't get behind.

- ❖ Lunch hour on a weekday
- ❖ After breakfast on Saturday morning
- ❖ Right after dinner on Mondays
- ❖ At Starbuck's, over coffee or chai tea
- ❖ On Tuesdays after the kids are in bed

You get the point. Choose your time and do it. Laura would tell you that the very process of tracking did wonders for her sense of control over her life. It will do the same for you.

Coaching Tip

You don't have to keep track of your spending forever. A few months will give you a feel for it. Once you know it in your bones, you can quit writing things down.

Finding Money

You're not likely to literally "find" money hidden in your home or under a rock in your front yard—although I do have a friend whose grandmother hid money and gold jewelry in her decorative pillows. The trouble is, the family didn't know it until *after* the estate sale. (Someone reading this book may indeed have money waiting for her in the red velvet sofa pillow!)

Most of us don't have jobs like Laura's or pockets that hold a few hundred dollars of tips each week. Still, we often have secret drawers in our spending, so to speak, that contain the money we say we don't have to save or invest. The trick—and it's not a difficult one—is to spot it.

By "finding money," I mean searching through your spending behavior to find ways to redirect your money. I call this the *latte theory* because it is the most common example of found money.

The latte theory says that if you give up or reduce the number of lattes you buy each week, you'll easily have enough money to invest each month. The level of sacrifice depends on how badly you want the dream that you have in mind.

Here are some other ideas (from Avis Pohl's *Everywoman's Money: Less Debt, More Cash*) that fit into the latte theory:

❖ Carry your lunch from home instead of always eating in a restaurant or cafeteria.

❖ Look for two-for-one or "early bird" specials if you eat in restaurants with friends who are also trying to save more money.

❖ Clip coupons. These are especially good when grocery stores offer double or triple coupon days.

❖ Wash your own car and pump your own gas. Some gas stations even give free car washes with gas purchases.

❖ Call your telephone long-distance carrier about every six months, and ask if you're getting the best rate offered for your kind of usage. The company will often offer an unpublished rate just to keep your business. You can get comparative information on a Web site called A Bell Tolls (www.abelltolls.com).

❖ Pay off your credit card balances each month. Paying only the minimum will keep your credit clean, but the interest continues to grow, and you'll find that the entire bill increases monthly even if you add no new purchases.

❖ Don't pay an annual fee for your credit cards.

❖ Do you really need cable TV? If you need it only for good reception, just get the basic plan.

❖ Have friends share rental movies, or check out videos from the library.

❖ Go to matinees to see new films.

❖ Ask for senior discounts if you're old enough. You'd be surprised at how often you get them.

❖ Clean your own house.

❖ Cook on weekends, and make your own frozen dinners.

❖ Mow your own lawn. It's good for your mind, your body, and your pocketbook.

❖ Carpool to work, or use city transportation and avoid parking costs.

❖ Buy monthly passes for buses and trains.

❖ Use a library instead of buying books or magazines.

❖ Never sign a credit card receipt without checking the purchase price(s). Those wonderful sale prices are not always scanned into the computer correctly.

❖ Walk or ride your bike instead of joining a gym or having a personal trainer.

❖ Look at your phone bill. Do you really need the extra line, caller ID, call waiting, and call forwarding?

❖ Do you really need a cellular phone? If so, are you paying for a more expensive plan than you really need?

❖ Do you need a different car, or will your old one still be fine for a few more years? Your insurance rate and licensing may go down as your car ages.

❖ Talk to an insurance agent to see if you have the best rate for the age of your car. Maybe you should drop the collision insurance now.

❖ Review your insurance policies annually. Have enough insurance to cover your needs, but not more than you need.

❖ If your old car is getting too expensive to maintain, buy a used car rather than a new one. The first two years of depreciation are the greatest.

❖ Do you get the extended warranty on many things you buy? Sometimes that is covered by the store where you purchased the item.

❖ Buy in quantity when it is cheaper, but pay attention to whether it really does save money.

❖ Shop for new clothes at outlet stores. You can trim your clothing budget by buying only what you really need.

❖ Plan your wardrobe around what you already have, and buy only what you need. If you have just a few blouses, you will wear them more often and finally either wear them out or get tired of them.

❖ Find a nice consignment shop to sell some of the clothes that you no longer wear, and shop for something that you really need while you're there.

❖ Donate things that you don't use or want, and get receipts to help lower your tax bill.

❖ Shop for Christmas all year long, and take advantage of sales.

❖ Make coffee at home, and save lattes for a special treat.

❖ Instead of buying lottery tickets, put the money into your interest-bearing cash reserve account. Your odds of winning are better.

❖ Buy generic brands of food and drug store items.

❖ Get a roommate, or rent a room in your home. If you rent to a student who won't be there all year long, you'll still have some privacy.

❖ Press your clothes at home if all they need is pressing, and save part of your dry cleaning bill.

❖ Check your insurance premiums. Get quotes online (www.Quotes.com) or from an insurance broker or agent to see if you can save some money on your premiums. You may get a better rate by having your home or renter's insurance with the same carrier as your auto insurance.

❖ If you need life insurance, buy term insurance and be a responsible investor with the money that you save over permanent insurance premiums. If no one is depending on you financially, you may not need life insurance at all. Check with your adviser.

❖ Save money in an interest-bearing account for big items such as furniture, and buy when you have the money instead of financing on credit.

❖ If you buy a seldom-used item such as a kitchen appliance, purchase less than the top-of-the-line model or brand if it will serve you well enough.

❖ Turn down your heat when you leave for the day to save on your heating bill.

❖ Never sign a document that you haven't read or don't understand.

❖ Don't be too proud to order from the children's menu if you find that restaurants serve you too much food.

❖ Keep your car on its scheduled maintenance so that it will last longer.

❖ Pay bills on time so that no late fees or interest are added.

❖ Research large items that you plan to buy on the Internet to save gas, time, and avoid falling for persuasive salespeople.

❖ Take enough cash from each paycheck to get you through that period, and avoid too many stops at the ATM. Keep track of where that cash is going.

The truth is, people who track their money closely are ahead of the pack, and they are also in the minority. With the advent of the automated teller machine, having access to your money is easier than ever. Debit cards, as convenient as they are, remove us one step further from really "seeing" where our money goes. In fact, it's causing havoc for many people. Most people are managing their finances by default. If you balance your checkbook by calling to get a balance on the phone or at the ATM machine, watch out. You're headed for some unpleasant surprises and probably a bit of trouble. If someone makes a mistake with your money, how will you know?

So, track what you earn and what you spend to find green in your financial "Where's Money?" picture.

Coaching Tip

Above all, make your spending count for something. You use your life energy to create money. You dishonor yourself if you throw your money away without thinking. Try not to make judgements about how you or others spend their money. If you really want something and you have the money, the cost is not particularly relevant. If you don't have the money to pay for it, the cost is still irrelevant.

Analyzing Your Spending Habits

While Laura may not have called her notebook a "cash flow analysis," that is exactly what it was. She analyzed her spending to see where her flow of cash went each month. It was revealing and helpful. I recall the first time that I analyzed my spending. I was surprised to see what I was really spending on eating out and buying clothes. My dry cleaning bill was too high as well.

The cash flow sheet in Appendix A, "Worksheets," shows how simple and helpful this step is.

Fitting Your Money into a Plan

If you have a budget, you will now want to compare the numbers on your spreadsheet with the projected amounts in your budget. Are you on track? Does your spending closely match your budget? If so, nice work. If not, you've got work to do.

If you don't have a budget, put one on your "To Do" list. It's another way to stay in control of your life.

Any budget has fixed expenses, such as your mortgage, car note, insurance, some utilities. While you can sometimes spring some money loose by renegotiating interest on loans, for example, it is the discretionary expenses such as groceries, clothing, entertainment, and gasoline that are changeable from month to month and that can wreak havoc on a budget. This is where you have the most flexibility to find money to invest.

When it comes to finding money, the budget is the treasure map. Laura compared her budget to her actual spending. She was spending more than she budgeted because she had never counted her tips as income. She had mentally ignored the tips as income because she could never be certain how much she would get in a given week. She simply spent it on "things" as she received it. Her cash flow analysis uncovered the tip money to be the fuel for her overspending on clothing and incidentals. She stopped it and saved the tips, and there it was: tuition and retirement.

As a self-employed woman who was relying on tips for two significant responsibilities instead of just relishing them as instant cash, Laura would need to keep at least six months of her income readily available in a money market account. I also advised her to make sure that she contributed to her retirement funds. Laura managed her cash flow closely to meet her objectives and stay on track. Let's summarize the process step by step:

1. Track your spending in a notebook. Enter what you purchase and how much it costs. Total the amounts daily.

2. At the end of the week, transfer those totals to a spreadsheet with categories that detail what specific areas you're spending the greatest percentage of your discretionary income on.

3. Compare the actual numbers to your budget, if you have one. If you don't have one, use the sample budget in this chapter to create one.

4. Determine whether you have a positive cash flow or a negative one. If it's positive, you have money to invest. If it's negative, you don't—yet.

5. Study your cash flow sheet and your budget to find available money to invest.

If you're spending more than you earn, you have a negative cash flow. If your credit card balances are also increasing, then you're in serious trouble. This debt can grow and strangle your ability to invest. Get help fast.

Here is an example of adjusting discretionary income so that you have money to invest.

Adjusting Discretionary Income to Create Investment Money

Expense	Cost Month	Alternative	Cost Month	Savings
Cable TV	$50	Movie rental (four)	$12	$38
Cell phone	$50	Pager	$10	$40
Health club	$60	Exercise equipment	$10	$50
Lunch	$120	Brown bag three days	$48	$72
Totals	$280		$70	$210

With a few simple shifts in spending, this person "found" more than $200 to invest each month.

I urge you to keep your adjustments realistic; you don't want to set yourself up for failure by a bare-bones approach, unless you are very motivated and disciplined to do it. Rather than eliminate an activity altogether, find a low-cost alternative. For example, rent a pager as your first line of information for about $10 a month. That way, you can decide whom to respond to and when from your cell phone. This will not only save you a lot of money, but it also will put you in control of your time.

It's all a trade-off. The question is, what are you willing to trade to find the money to invest? Maybe the following chart will help you decide.

What can an extra $200 a month accomplish? Let's do the math.

$200	Ten Years	Fifteen Years	Twenty Years	Thirty Years
8%	$36,000	$70,000	$118,000	$300,000
10%	$41,000	$84,000	$153,000	$455,000
12%	$46,000	$100,000	$199,000	$705,000

Creating Money That You Don't Have

Some women don't have enough money every month to cover the basics or are in some other way hindered from using money to invest. The challenge is real, and it is also doable. This is the true test of whether a person will do what she needs to do to be financially successful. Once you have gone through the tracking, cash flow sheet, and budget analysis, and determined that there is no money to be found, you may need to create extra income through increasing your job skills and salary, acquiring a part-time job, or starting a side business.

Increase Your Earning Power

If you are employed but not making enough money, you'll want to "up" your income by increasing your skills. Lifelong learning is an essential life skill. Changes in the marketplace are happening with lightning speed, and a person's skill set can rapidly become obsolete. Companies will often train you for a higher-paying position. Higher education no longer requires you to attend school during the day or even on campus. If you want to return to school, many universities now offer distance education and online learning. Although tuition has risen, it's easier than ever to fund your education with scholarships, loans, and grants. Visit www.petersons.com for information about online learning and www.finaid.org for financing your education.

One other thing: Find out from your supervisor what you can do to be promoted to a higher-paying position. Then do it, and remember to use at least part of your added income for investing, *after* contributing the maximum amount allowable to your 401(k).

Earn Extra

There are many ways to earn extra money. Remember, you don't need that much to invest each month. The more, the better, but start with what is in front of you.

Because you'll be earning money in addition to what you already do (whether working outside the home or in it), try to earn your investment money doing something easy, something in your natural skill set or passion.

Companies need part-time staff. Think about the businesses that you are in each week when you grocery shop, bank, shop, or work out. They know you already. Ask if they need part-time help. Who knows, maybe your gym will hire you in exchange for free membership. Then you can direct the money that you usually pay to be a member toward your investment plan.

Work for Yourself

Instead of working for someone else, you may want to work for yourself. Start simple.

Do work in your natural skill set or creative passion

For example, if you decorate beautifully for holidays, do it for money. If you paint rooms well or love to walk dogs, get paid for it. Are you good at planning trips, know how to teach canoeing, or cook special low-fat meals? Let people pay you to do it. Here are a few other ideas:

❖ Like throwing parties? Do it for friends and associates once or twice a month. Produce kids' birthday parties.

❖ Are you a natural organizer? Organize homes, garages, and closets.

❖ Love yardwork? Plant the bulbs that other women can't get to. Trim hedges or mow lawns for money and exercise.

❖ Are you a dessert lover? Make cheesecake and sell it to upscale coffee shops. Or, get friends to buy your dessert of the month.

❖ Are you an innovative cook? Sell your favorite recipes over the Internet.

❖ Know grammar? Edit manuscripts and reports.

❖ Like helping kids succeed? Tutor them.

Do work that parallels what you're already doing

For example, as long as you're running errands, run some for neighbors—for pay. Shop a lot? Be someone's shopper. Are you on the Atkins' Diet or another branded eating plan? Cook meals for friends on the same diet. Offer to videotape people's favorite shows on your VCR. Bake extra loaves of bread and deliver them still warm on week-ends to buyers in your neighborhood.

Apply your natural or developed skills to a clear need people have

For example, become an Internet expert and teach others how to use it. Fill scrapbooks and photo albums for busy families. Wash your neighbors' cars in their own driveways on Saturday mornings.

Whatever your talents are, you can pursue ways to develop them into an enterprise. Women are starting businesses every day in addition to their "day jobs." Eventually, the non–day job becomes their business. If you're ready for that, visit the Small Business Administration Web site to obtain the resources and explore the possibilities at www.sba. gov. You may want to visit the Web sites for Count Me In (www. count-me-in.org/) and Oyster (www.oysterfinancial.com) as well. Count Me In awards micro loans to women-owned small businesses, and Oyster has an excellent loan and information program for business owners.

Go!

The easy part is watching your money grow. The challenge is to find it and consistently invest it. Even that is made easier when you're doing it for something that you feel passionate about, like having enough to live without assistance, or to fund your child's education, or to buy a second home on the shore. Be tenacious. It's worth it.

In summary:

1. Buy your version of Laura's pink notebook.
2. Keep track of how much you spend and what you spend it on.
3. Develop a budget, and follow it.
4. Increase your income or reduce your expenses by making trade-offs.
5. Invest the leftovers.

If you do this, you will never regret it. So says Laura and the millions of other women investing every month.

The Bottom Line

Stop saying that you don't have enough money to invest. Start saying that you are taking steps to become a confident investor.

Reader's Journal:

Knowledge Gained:

_____
_____
_____
_____
_____
_____
_____
_____
_____
_____

Steps I Will Take:

_____
_____
_____
_____
_____
_____
_____
_____
_____
_____
_____

It was her first day on the job as a receptionist at a brokerage firm. Deborah wasn't really sure how she ended up in this place. The phones were ringing, and it was her job to answer and connect the parties to their "account executive." Every other call happened to be someone asking for a quote on a stock. "What's the last trade on IBM?" they would ask. "What's the market doing?" (This was way before you could get instant quotes on your computer or cell phone.) A machine that resembled a typewriter sat on her desk next to the phone. There was a black screen with numbers and letters that blinked and changed prices continually. It was her version of the Twilight Zone. She felt as if she were in another country. Were these people speaking English?

Gradually, Deborah began picking up the language of investing. Soon she was giving quotes on stocks, futures, and options. When someone called for the last trade on a stock, Deborah would give a thorough rundown. "IBM opened at 97, and the last trade was at 97¼; 250,000 shares have been traded so far." Not bad for someone who didn't know a stock from a bond when she walked in the door. It became fun.

After immersing herself in the intricacies of the stock market, Deborah knew that this was where she belonged. It was exciting, and she liked observing how wealth was made in America. After Deborah spent a few months answering the phones and working with the account executives, the office manager asked her if she would be interested in studying for her stockbroker's license.

The rest is history. I am the Deborah in this story. I remember thinking, "Hey, once you understand what all the investment terms mean, it isn't very complex at all."

Chapter 7

The Language of Investing

The Bottom Line

Learn the language of investing, and you will understand the world of investing.

Every profession develops its own language. Outsiders feel a bit like aliens when they hear it. Hearing people speak a language that you don't understand can be intimidating but also fascinating.

When I entered the investment industry, I was struck by how complex a relatively simple process was made to appear. There are a number of reasons for this, in my opinion. First, when you're on the inside looking out, things do seem clearer. You adopt phrases and codes that make sense to others using the language but little sense to those unfamiliar with it. Second, I think that the industry has enjoyed making its work mysterious. After all, if people don't understand what you're saying, you've got an edge over them. If they don't understand the language and the process, they have to rely on you and what you know. You become indispensable. They need you, and for the most part, they don't question you. This is called job security.

Well, those days are becoming extinct, not only in the financial industry, but in every industry, including medicine and law. Today, people are sophisticated consumers, and they don't put up with intimidating know-it-alls. The Information Age and the Internet are calling every industry to a new level of openness and partnership with consumers.

Talking Money

Talking money is a new experience for many women. We've been closed-mouthed about it. Investing wasn't our world. We've talked shopping and good buys and allowances, not stocks, bonds, and securities. But talking about investments as easily as we talk about the Olympics or this season's palette of fashion colors is where we are headed as women.

I find that many clients still feel it is impolite to ask anyone about their financial dealings. They don't have other women in their lives who openly discuss investments, so they don't ask questions or engage in open discussion about it. There is still a significant amount of apprehension and even shame associated with not knowing about investments. We feel stupid that we don't know, and we feel stupid if we ask, and so we are silent. We tiptoe quietly around the topic and exit the discussion. What we don't realize is that exiting the discussion can leave us out of the money loop in the future.

Happily, it's a new day for women and investing, and millions of us not only speak investing as a language, we also use it to create assets that we will live on when our great-great-grandchildren are joining us for sherry on the veranda.

Is learning the language of investing difficult? Not really. Does it take time? Not so much time for the basics, a little more time for the advanced lingo. You'll learn how to carry on a basic investment conversation in this chapter.

Bring someone else in on your investment language quest. Ask your kids—or your sister, your aunt, or your mother—to quiz you on the terms. Make learning investments "the new thing to do." It will lead to a new consciousness about money and investing, which will lead to a new set of attitudes and behaviors, and suddenly you'll be talking investments over coffee as though you've known the language all your life.

Market Talk

There is a glossary in this book that gives you a concise description of investment terms. You'll want to study it and have someone quiz you on the terms. This chapter, however, is about the language of investing—using those terms in conversation. It will help you talk investments and understand the conversations about them.

Suppose you're at a lunch counter and you hear the couple next to you talking about investments.

She says, "How's the market doing today?"

He says, "It's up three quarters!"

She says, "Did you hear how Cisco's doing?"

He says, "I'm not sure. I had to leave the office before the market report came on TV."

She says, "I'll check it on the Internet when I get back. I want to buy more of it when it goes down a bit."

He says, "Have you put a limit order on it?"

She says, "No, not yet. I put a day order on it last week, but it didn't hit the numbers I wanted."

He says, "I did another trade online this morning."

She says, "Really? You're really getting into that online trading, aren't you?"

He says, "Everyone around me is doing it, so I thought I'd try it."

She says, "Chuck's not liking that so much, I'll bet."

He says, "Well, hey, what can I say? We still need him, but we can venture off on our own when the urge strikes us."

She says, "Yeah, I've done a few online trades myself lately. Made us some money."

He says, "Really? Have you lost any money?"

She says, "What do you mean, 'lost any'? You know we're in it for the long haul. The stock may go down, but we're not losing money."

This is a typical exchange among investors. What were they talking about? Let me tell you.

"How's the Market Doing Today?"

By "market," most people mean the stock market. They're asking whether the prices of stocks are up or down. In other words, are more people buying stocks today, or are more people selling stocks today? If more people are buying than selling, the market is "up"; if more people are selling than buying, the market is "down."

The market is made up of companies who have chosen to sell pieces of ownership to others, to people like you and me in direct or roundabout ways. Those pieces of ownership are called shares of stock.

Those companies trade on exchanges where stock is—you guessed it—exchanged. The largest and oldest stock exchange in the United States (dating from 1794) is the New York Stock Exchange (NYSE). Companies trading on the NYSE meet stiff requirements for their stock to be listed and traded there. The American Stock Exchange is the second-largest exchange in the country. Both of these are floor-based exchanges. There are also regional stock exchanges that were originally created to sell the stocks of local companies.

Regional Exchanges	Location
1. Pacific Exchange	San Francisco, Los Angeles
2. Philadelphia Exchange	Philadelphia
3. Chicago Stock Exchange (formerly the Midwest Stock Exchange)	Chicago
4. Intermountain Stock Exchange	Salt Lake City

The term "stock" originally meant just that: livestock. Wall Street (and there used to truly be a wall there) was the place livestock was bought and sold.

The New York Stock Exchange, located on Wall Street, was established in front of a buttonwood tree in New York where a group of 10 wealthy businessmen traded "stock" and eventually went on to finance America's railroads and other industries.

Another market where stocks trade is the NASDAQ Stock Market. NASDAQ is a major national and international stock market that uses computers and telecommunications to make its trades. Similar to the NYSE, companies must meet listing requirements to trade in this market. The NASDAQ Stock Market is where several large companies such as Microsoft and Intel trade.

Some companies don't trade on the stock exchange often because they cannot meet the capitalization requirements. The capitalization is simply the price of a company's shares times the number of shares outstanding. Ideally, the smaller the company the lower their market capitalization. The market capitalization does not always reflect a company's value. These companies are usually smaller and carry more investment risk. Investments in these companies are made over the counter (OTC). Remember, the over-the-counter market is where stocks of companies that are "unlisted" trade. An unlisted stock belongs to a company that does not meet the financial requirements to be listed on the larger exchanges. We'll discuss these terms more fully in Chapter 8, "How to Invest in Stocks."

"It's Up Three Quarters"

Investors want to know *on average* how the companies in the stock market are doing. Are they increasing in value or dropping in value? The easiest way to answer is to select a few companies that represent the whole and average their performance. This average indicates how the market in general is doing. The companies that are used in this averaging are called *indicators*.

The most popular indicators are the Dow Jones Industrial Average and the Standard & Poor 500. When you hear "The Dow is up 4 points," you know that the value of the 30 companies that the Dow uses to average the market's performance is up an average of 4 points. When you hear, "The S&P 500 is up 4 points," you know that the value of the 500 companies that Standard & Poor uses to average the market's performance is up an average of 4 points.

Often, when a person asks how the market is doing, she is asking how the Dow is doing. The Dow is a snapshot of the market's activity.

Dow Jones and Standard & Poor choose the companies on their lists carefully and make changes infrequently. As our country moves from primarily industrial companies such as U.S. Steel to service companies such as Gateway, you'll see the lists reflect that shift. Industrial companies on the list are replaced by service companies to more accurately reflect the evolving market.

Look for the Dow Jones and S&P 500 in your newspaper or online. Or, tune in to a network such as CNBC and listen for mention of these two indicators. It's a standard in the language of investments.

So, back to the conversation that you overheard at lunch. When she asked how the market was doing and he answered, "It's up three quarters," he was probably referring to a Dow Jones report, the most commonly used indicator.

"Did You Hear How Cisco's Doing?"

The woman in the conversation has her eye on one company in particular. She wants to invest in the company, but she wants to do it on her terms, as much as possible. In this case, she's looking at Cisco, a popular technology company with a solid performance history.

Like all companies on the stock exchange, Cisco went through some big hoops to get permission to sell off shares to investors. That process is called "going public." When a company meets the requirements to go public, the buzz is on. Investors hear it coming, and if it's a big company with a long history of success, they'll line up to buy stock the moment it is available. Just before it goes public so that investors like you and me can purchase stock in the company, the company offers options to buy stock to the privileged few whom they have either struck a deal with or who have helped the company succeed in some other way.

Let's say that the company has been valued at $25 million and is issuing a million shares of stock at $25 a share. Those privileged few get to buy the stock at $25 a share. Then the company goes public, or makes its "initial public offering" (IPO) to the rest of us. People clamor to buy it—and the more who buy, the higher the stock price rises. This is what happened to Cara when she bought her UPS stock (see Chapter 4, "What Is Investing?"). The more people want a certain stock, the more valuable it is.

Most companies never go public. They are funded by private investors or by the profits that they make selling products or services.

"I'll Check It on the Internet"

The Internet is an investor's dream, enabling you to find out virtually anything about a publicly traded company. As you become an experienced investor, you'll narrow down a few sites as your favorites. You learn your way around the site and can find out the information you want.

Many Web sites are the online reach of brokerage houses with a real address and building, called "brick-and-mortar companies"; others are solely Internet brokerages. A brokerage house is simply a company of brokers who make trades on the stock exchange. You will have a relationship with a stockbroker and brokerage house either directly or indirectly through your financial planner.

Two of my favorite brokerage sites are these:

- ❖ **financialmuse.com**—A site for women that includes excellent information and education
- ❖ **charlesschwab.com**—A site that includes a learning center and a special section for women investors

There are hundreds of sites like this. Find your own favorites and get familiar with them.

"Have You Put a Limit Order on It?"

I like this part of investing because it gets you just what you want when you want it. It's very simple.

With a limit order, you tell your broker that you want to buy a stock, but only under certain conditions. In this case, the woman had a limit in her mind of what she would be willing to pay. If she put a limit order on her purchase of Cisco, her broker would watch the stock, and when it lowered to the price she would pay, would buy it automatically.

You can place other types of orders on the stocks that you want to buy:

- ❖ **Day order:** The limits that you put on a stock are good only for a day. In other words, if the woman told her broker that she wanted Cisco only if it went down to a certain point *that day,* the broker would not buy it for her the next day.

❖ **Good to cancel order:** This means that the woman wants her order for Cisco to be ongoing until she cancels it.

❖ **Market order:** If the woman put a market order on Cisco, she is willing to pay whatever the market bears to get it.

"I Did Another Trade Online This Morning"

Trading stock of individual companies is time-consuming and sometimes not as profitable as investing in a mutual fund, where a number of companies' stocks are traded together. However, if you have the time, stomach, and money to do it, trading individual stocks is fascinating—possibly even addictive.

A rather new phenomenon in investing is online trading. Originally, this took the traditional financial services industry by surprise, but it quickly caught up. Most brokerage services will give an investor the choice to buy direct or through a broker.

It's up to you, but do use the Internet for researching companies and tracking how stocks have done. If you have concerns about how online firms conduct business you can visit www.gomez.com. This Web site is the *Consumer Reports* of online business.

"Have You Lost Any Money?"

This question is one that is rarely asked among experienced investors. They invest for the long haul, as a rule, and know when to stay in and when to get out.

To an experienced investor, a stock may "go down," but that doesn't mean that the person has lost money. A confident investor will stay in until the stock makes money, even if it takes 10 years or more. If a stock "tanks," meaning that a company goes under, the investor will get out; otherwise, she hangs in there.

Coaching Tip

Don't marry your stocks. Cut your losses and move on. This is particularly true if you own the stock of the company where you work.

Other Phrases You'll Hear

You'll hear certain investment phrases nearly every day if you watch television, listen to the radio, or are around people who invest.

"What's the Volume of Shares?"

"Volume" refers either to the total number of shares traded on a given day in all markets or to the total number of shares traded on a given day by a particular company. It shows how active the market is. A great deal of activity or a small amount of activity gets attention.

"The 52-Week High (or Low)"

This phrase refers to the highest and lowest price that a stock has traded over the past 52 weeks. It helps investors know where the current price fits into the recent overall pattern of a stock's activity. This number changes every day, of course, as today is added and a year ago today is dropped off.

"The Earnings Report Is Good (Bad, Questionable, Inconclusive)"

An earnings report, also known as the earnings per share report, is the amount of earnings, or profits, of a company divided by the number of shares of stock that are outstanding. Those who analyze stock (analysts) use the earnings report to assess how well a company is performing.

"Its P/E Is 19"

When someone talks about P/E, she means the price earning ratio. The P/E ratio is the price of a stock divided by its earnings per share. The ratio is used to give an investor an idea of how much she is paying for the "earnings" of the stock. During the Internet stock craze, P/Es were irrelevant because the companies had no earnings. An average P/E is 25. If a company's P/E is really high, such as 100, it means either that there is great demand or that the company is expected to grow a lot in the future. The higher the P/E, the higher the risk and potential reward, in most cases. For example, say America Online has a P/E ratio of 99 or is currently trading at 99 times earnings as of the close of business today, whereas another company is trading at a P/E of 29. Investors must believe that America Online has a lot more earnings in its future.

Coaching Tip

If a P/E ratio is 25, you must be willing to pay $25 for every dollar that company is earning today. If the P/E ratio is 50, you must be willing to pay $50 for every dollar that company is earning today. The higher the P/E, the riskier the investment because you're counting on the company to be very profitable in the future. The P/E is also called "times earnings" or "the multiple."

"I Saw It in the 'Value Line'"

Investors look to the "Value Line Investment Survey" as the Bible of stock research. You can find virtually anything about a company if it is followed. The survey includes historical data, performance data, management team information, and a rating by analysts of whether the stock is a strong buy or one that should be held or sold.

"I Invest Primarily in Blue Chips"

This means that the investor has most of her investment dollars in solid, tried-and-true companies that keep growing and issuing dividends. These are also called "large caps." "Blue chip" was derived from the blue chip in poker—the most valuable chip. Blue chips include companies such as General Electric, Gillette, Citibank, and hundreds of others.

"Morningstar Ranked It Seventh"

The "Morningstar Mutual Fund Report" is the Bible for mutual fund investors. It is a two-page research report that ranks mutual fund performance by a one- to five-star rating. The rankings are conducted every quarter. Because you are, or will become, an investor in mutual funds, I suggest that you review the report and visit the Morningstar Web site at www.morningstar.com. The Morningstar Mutual Fund Rankings are readily accessible at your local library.

"AAR Predicts Good Things for That Company"

The average annual return (AAR) is a measure of how an investment has performed over periods of time. Performance is measured over a month, a quarter, a year, and increments of 3, 5, and 10 years. This gives an investor a sense of what the average performance has been on an annualized basis.

"She Prefers to Invest in Mutual Funds"

Mutual funds are popular because they allow investors to invest smaller amounts of money and still have diversification and professional money management. In a nutshell, a mutual fund is an investment that pools the money of several investors. A professional money manager is responsible for deciding which specific individual securities to invest in. There are different types of mutual funds just as there are different types of investments. You will base your choice on what it is you want, growth or income.

Coaching Tip

If you have less than $100,000 to invest, you should invest through mutual funds. Otherwise, you won't have enough diversification.

"He Placed a Trade for Me"

"Placing a trade" means that you've placed an order for a particular stock. The order states how many shares you want to buy and at what price. Here's how it works:

1. You order 100 shares of Verizon from your stockbroker.
2. Your stockbroker calls the order in to the trading desk.
3. The trading desk notifies the broker on the floor of the exchange.
4. The broker on the floor buys the shares and notifies the desk what it cost.
5. The desk calls your stockbroker.
6. Your stockbroker calls you to report the price and to confirm that the order was placed.

This process can take a matter of seconds from beginning to end.

Investors can also do this on their own from their personal computers or wireless phones or personal assistants.

"Their Stock Symbol Is PG"

A ticker, or stock symbol, is the code that you find in stock market reports. It's the string of initials running across your television screen during the market news. It's the way you find the stocks or funds that you invest in on the stock exchange. If a company's symbol is four letters or more, it trades on the NASDAQ or over the counter.

"The Last Price Was 16½"

This means that the last price that a stock sold for on a given day was $16.50.

"It Has a Small (or Medium or Large) Market Cap"

Companies have market caps, or a market value that is calculated by this simple formula: Number of shares × current market price of the shares. In general, the market cap indicates the size and performance of a company.

Coaching Tip

Learning the language of money is the most important thing you can do. You are limited or set free by your ability to understand the concepts in your own language.

It's fun to understand the language of money! The words are used over and over again, as in any industry.

Ida's Process

When Ida discovered that she needed to invest more aggressively, she went to the library to research some stocks and mutual funds that she could invest in through her employer and on her own. She used the "Value Line Investment Survey" and "Morningstar Mutual Fund Report." From this research, she was able to determine that she did not want to initially invest in individual stocks. It would have required a substantial amount of money, and she would not have had a diversified, or varied, portfolio. Plus, she sensed that researching individual stocks required more knowledge than she had at that time.

Coaching Tip

When you diversify, you reduce your volatility and risk of loss. Ninety-two percent of investment returns depend upon the asset allocation. What percentage of your overall investments are in stocks, bonds, or cash?

The Morningstar guides enabled her to get a good sense of how the funds offered by her employers had performed. In it, she was also able to "meet" the portfolio managers through their resumés, which increased her confidence. Most important, she was able to see a graph that illustrated exactly how much $10,000 invested would have grown in 10 years. The numbers and concepts were no longer abstract to her. This was actual performance.

Based on her own research, Ida was able to make an informed decision about where to invest her money. Ida was learning to speak the language of investing, and today she talks investments with the best of them—just like you will.

The Bottom Line

Speaking the language of investing will prepare you to buy your financial future.

Reader's Journal:

Knowledge Gained:

_____

_____

_____

_____

_____

_____

_____

_____

_____

Steps I Will Take:

_____

_____

_____

_____

_____

_____

_____

_____

_____

*A*ngela had risen through the ranks of her high-tech company at a steady clip. She was investing the maximum amount allowable in her 401(k) retirement plan and was investing in an employee stock option program through a payroll deduction. Her employee stock option program now represented more than 25 percent of her overall portfolio. The share price had recently sunk to its lowest point for the year, and she was questioning whether she should sell or buy more. She decided this might be a good time to explore other stock alternatives.

Angela was very knowledgeable about the telecommunications industry and had been contemplating investing in some of her company's suppliers. A stockbroker referred to her by a colleague suggested that she sell all the company stock she owned and invest the proceeds into stock and mutual funds that he recommended. Angela listened to his advice but didn't follow it. She felt that the tax implications weren't in her best interest.

Instead, she got some friends together and formed an investment club. Through it, her portfolio experienced impressive growth. The broker who provided her club with the research and knowledge that it needed to get started ultimately became her broker.

Angela is now an experienced investor and usually invests on her own, but she maintains an account with her broker. If she does her own research, she uses a discount brokerage account; if not, she lets her adviser do the research and place the order.

Angela has created an investment pattern that suits her. She listens to suggestions but ultimately resists what doesn't match her knowledge and instincts. She credits the investment club with strengthening her understanding of investing as well as her portfolio.

Chapter 8

How to Invest in Stocks

The Bottom Line

Investing in stocks is an essential investment strategy and how you build wealth.

Your portfolio, or the assortment of investment products that you purchase, needs to include stocks to be well-balanced. The amount and type of stocks that you purchase is up to you, as is the type of ownership, and the choices are not difficult to determine.

There are two advantages to buying stocks. First, if you're investing for growth, stocks give you a way to make your money grow—in other words, they provide capital appreciation. Second, if you are more of an income-oriented, or bond, investor, stocks compensate for inflation, hedging against it. In other words, if you invest in bonds to receive income, inflation may take a bite out of that income. Investing in stocks can provide the money to help you overcome the impact of inflation. The two work together.

Stocks, or equities, represent an ownership interest in a company, and it is through your ownership that you can expect to get growth from your investment (capital gains) and a share of the corporate profits (dividends). (If you're looking for immediate income from your investments, see Chapter 9, "How to Invest in Bonds.") Even when you are retired and looking to your portfolio for income, you will probably still need some stocks to help you keep up with inflation.

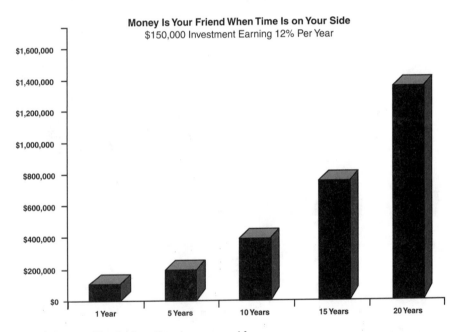

Money is your friend when time is on your side.

You can own stocks in several different ways. You can choose the stocks yourself or in conjunction with an adviser, you can have a private portfolio manager select them for you, or you can use a mutual fund. Angela chose the stocks herself with the occasional help of an adviser.

How Stocks Make Money for You

Stock ownership gives you two ways to make money: dividends and capital gains.

Dividends

If you own stock, you own part of a company—say, Microsoft. As an owner, dividends are your share of the company's profits. Dividends are declared by the board of directors and are paid out to shareholders on a specified date each quarter. Many companies pride themselves on the fact that they pay regular dividends, have done so for years, and have raised their dividends on a regular basis.

Dividends are declared per share. Let's say that you own 100 shares of Microsoft, and the company declares a dividend of 10¢ per share, payable to shareholders of record on May 31, 20**, to be paid on June 30, 20**. First of all, you have to own the stock on May 31 to receive the dividend. If you do, you will receive $10 on June 30 (100 shares × 10¢ per share). Pay attention to the price information in your newspaper when a company that you're thinking of buying is close to a dividend payment. You'll see a term called the "ex-date." This is the first date when a buyer would not receive the dividend—in this case, June 1.

At the end of the year, you will receive a Form 1099, which reports to you and to the IRS how much you were paid in dividends for the year. You must report this income and pay taxes on it each year. Dividends are taxed as regular income (28 percent, 31 percent, 33 percent, 36 percent, or 39.6 percent federal), which is a higher rate than the long-term capital gains rate (20 percent federal—see the next section). Any state income would be in addition to the federal tax. So some investors, especially those in the higher tax brackets, may not particularly want a stock to pay dividends.

Remember, not all companies pay dividends. For instance, technology and other high-growth companies most frequently choose to reinvest their earnings back into the company. Any earnings that a company does not pay out to shareholders are called "retained earnings."

Capital Gains

Capital gains are what most people think of when they think of stocks. Let's look at an example: Say that you buy 100 shares of a company for $30 per share. That's a total purchase price of $3,000, not including transaction costs. If the value goes up to $50 per share, your investment is now worth $5,000. If you sell at that point, you would have a capital gain of $2,000 ($5,000 − $3,000 = $2,000). It is important that you keep track of your cost basis—the total amount that you paid for a stock—so that you can properly report your capital gains. There are two types of capital gains: short-term and long-term. The difference is in the way you are taxed. Short-term gains are taxed as ordinary income. Long-term gains are taxed at a maximum rate of 20 percent.

Coaching Tip

You don't have to keep track of your cost basis in an IRA. You do need to know what your after-tax contribution is to a traditional IRA if you didn't deduct it from your income taxes.

Where Stocks Trade

Stocks trade on a variety of exchanges—both national and regional. In the previous chapter, we discussed the New York Stock Exchange (NYSE) and the AMEX/NASDAQ. Most of the stocks you will likely be considering will trade on one of these two exchanges. Each of these exchanges has its own nickname:

New York Stock Exchange	The Street
American Stock Exchange	The Curb
NASDAQ	Over the Counter

There are also a variety of regional exchanges in places such as Boston, Philadelphia, and Chicago. These exchanges often specialize in a particular type of stock and will establish an index to measure it. For example, Philadelphia has the Semiconductor Index. Chicago is known for its futures and options trading.

For companies with lower levels of investor interest, there are the "pink sheets." Stocks trading here tend to be low-priced (below $5 per share) and are often penny stocks. Penny stocks often have a share price of less than $1. While legitimate companies may have stocks priced that low, many companies offering penny stocks are unscrupulous. Stocks traded here also tend to have very low daily volume. Only a few shares a day will actually change hands. Because there is no way of verifying stock prices, it is difficult to determine actual prices. The market capitalization of these companies is small, and therefore they can't meet the listing requirements of the large stock exchanges. You can check for fraud by visiting the Securities and Exchange Commission Web site at www.sec.gov or www.stockdetective.com. Buyer beware!

Coaching Tip

Don't buy penny stocks. I don't think you should buy a stock that sells for less than $10 unless it is a good, solid company that has been beaten up lately and you believe it can come back. Penny stocks are just too risky.

There are exchanges in other countries as well, such as France, Germany, Hong Kong, Japan, and Mexico. This is where the shares of companies based in those countries would trade. However, for better-known foreign firms, their stocks may also be available on the NYSE in the form of "American Depository Receipts," or "ADRs." This is a convenience mechanism to make foreign shares with a large degree of investor interest more easily accessible. Before you dismiss the idea of investing in foreign companies, take a look at some of the products you use. You may be surprised at how many of them are produced by non-U.S. companies. For instance, did you know that companies in the following countries make these products?

Product	Company	Country
Whopper	Burger King	United Kingdom
Lucky Strike cigarettes	British American Tobacco	United Kingdom
Red Man chewing tobacco	Swedish Match AB	Sweden
Lea & Perrins	Groupo Danone	France
Rolls Royce	Volkswagen/BMW	Germany
LensCrafters	Luxottica Group	France
Shell gasoline	Royal Dutch Petroleum	Netherlands
Columbia Pictures	Sony	Japan

(continued)

Product	Company	Country
Stouffer's Lean Cuisine	Nestle	Switzerland
Hawaiian Punch	Cadbury Schweppes	United Kingdom
Jeep	Daimler Chrysler	Germany
Frigidaire refrigerators	Electrolux PLC	Sweden
7-11 Convenience Stores	Southland Corporation	Japan
Ben & Jerry's Ice Cream	Unilever NV	United Kingdom
Maybelline	L'Oreal ADR	France
Gerber baby food	Novartis AG	Switzerland
Dove soap	Unilever PLC	Netherlands
Los Angeles Dodgers	News Corporation	Australia

Market Capitalization

Market capitalization, or market cap, is simply the number of shares of stock outstanding multiplied by the closing price of that stock. For example, if Nokia has one million shares of stock outstanding and closed at $100 per share yesterday, then it has a market cap of $100 million. (Shares that are issued are outstanding shares until they are reacquired, redeemed, converted, or canceled by the company.)

Market caps are divided into brackets to differentiate large, medium, and small firms. There are also "mega-cap" and "micro-cap" stocks that represent the biggest of the large caps and the smallest of the small caps. Be careful as you use these descriptors because it seems that everyone has a different definition of each cap size. Use the numbers offered here as a general rule of thumb, and be sure to confirm what your information sources are using as their definitions.

Large-Cap Companies

Market cap: Usually $5 billion and up

This tends to be where you find your "blue-chip" companies. These are firms that have been around long enough and are established enough to have definitive market share, relatively stable profits, and often a history of paying dividends. The names of these firms are usually easily recognized, and you probably use their products and services in your daily life.

Large-Caps	Market Capitalization
Coca Cola	154,521,814,375
McDonald's	210,541,000,000
Ford	48,235,503,000
Wal-Mart	210,541,000,000

Mid-Cap Companies

Market cap: Usually between $1 billion and $5 billion

You may recognize some of these companies' names as well, but as the name implies, these firms are a bit smaller than their larger counterparts. Sometimes they're large companies whose stock price is currently depressed, while others are former small-cap companies that are successfully expanding and increasing their stock price, the number of shares outstanding, or both.

Mid-Caps	Market Capitalization
Wendy's	2,653,805,000
Kmart	2,790,575,000
Herman Miller	1,944,000,000
Abercrombie & Fitch	2,526,986,000

Small-Cap Companies

Market cap: Usually under $1 billion

This is one of the most aggressive of the size types, second only to micro-caps (a.k.a. penny stocks). Many small company stocks tend to have small "floats," meaning that there aren't many shares of stock out there in the first place, and many of them are "thinly traded," meaning that a very small number of shares is traded on a daily basis. This can make it difficult for a stock's price to appreciate much beyond the small daily volume.

If there aren't that many shares changing hands, it reduces the liquidity of your investment. If you wanted to sell your stock there might not be a buyer. Many companies start out as small-caps and grow into large-caps. Some companies are mismanaged, become unprofitable, and become small-caps. I can remember when Chrysler Company stock fell to $3 in the early 1980s and MCI Communications (now WorldCom) sold for $7 a share. Apple Computer sold for less than $10 a few years a go. Priceline.com sold for more than $100 a share in the past year and is now selling for $3.25. Priceline.com plummeted from a large-cap to a micro-cap in less than 52 weeks.

Small-Caps	Market Capitalization
Columbia Sportwear	994,000,000
Priceline.com	542,000

How to Choose a Stock

There are several schools of thought about how to choose stocks successfully. Just as fashion, diets, or business models go in and out of favor, so do stock selection philosophies. One year, the fashion is short skirts, the next year it's long skirts, and the next year it's pants! But when the fashion is pants, do you throw out all your skirts? No! Think about your stocks the same way. One year, large-cap growth is in fashion, the next it's small-cap growth, and the next it's international stocks. You have no idea what's going to be in fashion next.

To participate in the growth of a "hot" area, you obviously have to own something in that area. But that doesn't mean that you throw out everything else and own just one type of stock. Choosing stock is like choosing behaviors to match a situation. You'll probably want some that are defensive, some that are aggressive, and some that are good old everyday stocks.

Let's review some of these ideas and the types of companies that you will be dealing with.

Fundamental Investment Selection Styles

There is a set of "styles" that describe your goals as an investor. Read them and use those that fit your investment goals at a given time.

Growth Investing

In this style of investing, dividends are not as important as growth. What is important is how quickly a stock is growing. To measure this, you could look at things such as earnings growth, market-share growth, revenue growth, or new product growth. You may not want to simply look at the growth rate, but also to look at the acceleration rate of the growth.

Momentum Investing

A subset of growth investing is momentum investing. Here, you look to take advantage of a groundswell of interest that will carry your particular stock along for the ride with the other stocks in an industry sector or other group.

Value Investing

Value investing is almost the opposite of growth. Here, you're looking for the "Kmart blue-light specials" of the market, stocks whose prices have dropped but that still represent fundamentally good companies. This takes patience because you may have to wait a fair amount of time to see the kind of results you're looking for—but it is usually worth it.

Sector Rotation Investing

The market is divided into 10 major industry classifications, or sectors:

1. Consumer durables
2. Consumer staples
3. Energy
4. Financials
5. Health
6. Industrial cyclicals
7. Retail
8. Services
9. Technology
10. Utilities

Sector rotation means moving from one industry to another, depending on what sectors are expected to do well during the upcoming period of time. For instance, you would move into retail stocks when they are poised to report good earnings. When they move to a period of lighter sales, you would sell. You would then move into the sector that your indicators point to as the next market opportunity.

Checkbook Investing

This is a simple but frequently used way of deciding what stocks to include in a portfolio. The idea is to go through your checkbook and credit card statements and then select your stocks based on where you actually spend your own money. In a sense, it's your opportunity to make back some of the money that you spend with certain firms.

Technical Analysis

Technical analysis is a way of selecting stocks by studying the chart patterns of stock prices. Technical analysts believe that these charts point to patterns of behavior that indicate whether a stock is strong or on the verge of falling apart. Several different types of charts that can be plotted: time and price, point and figure, and Japanese candlewicking, to name a few.

Many people use a combination of fundamental and technical analysis. The fundamental analysis is used to figure out what to buy, and the technical analysis is used to determine whether this is a good time to buy or sell.

Day Trading and Market Timing

Day trading and market timing have been the subject of a great deal of media attention recently. They are undoubtedly highly aggressive, highly speculative styles of trading, and therefore potentially highly profitable. But I caution you strongly, even vehemently, against attempting these forms of portfolio management. You may recall from some of the news stories that many, many people have lost substantial amounts of money this way. Remember, the stock market is a long-term entity. No one knows what stocks are going to do on a minute-by-minute, hour-by-hour, or day-by-day basis. If you actually make money on a trade, consider it luck, and quit while you're ahead.

Think of it this way: If someone had figured out how to do this successfully by now, then every investor would be investing this way. And they don't. The wealthiest individuals and families in the world buy quality stocks and have them professionally managed.

Where to Go to Buy Stocks

Where you go to buy stocks depends on the kind of service you want. If you want advice, help with research, and someone to counsel you, find a good full-service broker. Most full-service brokers give you access to do your trades over the phone with them or through the Internet.

If you're more of a do-it-yourselfer, you may be happier with a discount brokerage firm. Sometimes there are brokers you can talk to, and sometimes not, depending on the firm. Because the research and the results are your responsibility, commissions are discounted. Fee-based accounts are not generally available from discounters.

How to Pay for Stock Transactions

You pay for your stock transactions, or trades, in one of two ways: by commission or by fee. With commissions, you pay by the trade. Obviously, a full-service commission will be more expensive than a discount commission. The additional cost goes to compensate your adviser for the research and counsel that she provides you.

With fees, you pay a percentage of the assets in the account instead of a commission for each trade. Most fee-based accounts allow for a fairly liberal number of trades. But don't expect to trade daily in an account like this. Day trading is considered highly speculative, and many firms will shut off trading privileges if they perceive that you are trading excessively.

A Word on IPO Investing

I introduced the subject of IPOs in Chapter 7, "The Language of Investing." IPOs are initial public offerings, or equity syndicate offerings. Here, a company that has never had stock traded in the market first makes it available. IPOs have a reputation for going up wildly, and everyone wants shares. But IPOs are a highly aggressive way to participate in the market, meaning that there is the potential for great loss as well as great profit. They do *not* all go up 1,000 percent the first day, but the ones that do most certainly make the news. You probably even know a few of them by name. Ivillage.com went public and doubled in value the first day. If you bought some of those shares, I'll bet that you joined in on the talk at the neighborhood barbecue about how the stock rocketed up on opening day. Many investors tell the front end of the story but forget to mention the fact that they bought only 10 shares, and that they got so wrapped up in the hype that they didn't sell when the stock took a tumble a few weeks later. Ivillage. com now trades at a little over $2 dollars a share.

Coaching Tip

There are different types of IPOs. "Hot issues" are snapped up by the institutional managers and rich individual investors. "Sticky issues" are available to small investors who might be unsophisticated. The bottom line on IPOs is this: If you are not a big investor and you have access to an IPO, you don't want it. It means that all the professional money managers and savvy investors passed on the opportunity. You don't want an IPO you can have.

Here's a word of advice, based on experience. You're going to want to get in on IPO stock. Most investors do. But understand that there's a pecking order at firms that do IPO deals. Some inexperienced investors believe that they're entitled to as many shares as they want of only the "good" deals. They demand IPO deals from their investment representatives. Don't do it. The IPO market has its own set of unique requirements for investors. Clients who have supported all of the firm's offerings will probably get more generous amounts of stock directed to them. Clients who have significant portfolios and who pay significant asset-management fees will also probably get more generous IPO allocations. And many times, nearly the entire IPO will go to institutional clients (mutual funds, pension funds, and the like). Understand where you fit in the hierarchy, and set your expectations accordingly.

If your investment representative's firm is not the lead underwriter on a particular deal, it's virtually impossible for the firm to get you shares of another firm's IPO. Remember, when companies go public they hire investment bankers to market the stock to investors. The investment bankers agree to pay the company a certain price per share or "underwrite" the deal. The investment bankers then distribute the shares to other investment firms or at a higher price and make money on the transaction.

Think about it. If you were in charge of a new issue that everyone wanted, wouldn't you keep all the shares at your own firm for your own clients? Of course you would. And Wall Street is no different.

Also know that on especially "hot" deals—the ones that are hyped up in the popular media—your investment representative may not get any shares for her clients at all. If this is the case, don't hold a grudge. Go to work on the next issue.

As an individual investor, if you don't rate as much IPO stock as you would like, consider having one of those institutional clients work for you by owning a mutual fund that participates in a lot of IPOs. Several participate to a fair degree, and a few focus on IPOs in particular.

If investing were a "get-rich-quick" activity, everyone would be billionaires! This is not to say that an occasional success story isn't possible. However, because no one holds that crystal ball, investing is in some ways a game of chance. Even an investor buying only the very best of company stock can lose money if the company experiences a setback or the economy or market has a downturn. There is no such thing as "guaranteed growth" or "guaranteed return" when investing in stock.

Investing should be seen as a long-term proposition. The longer an investor maintains a diversified stock portfolio, the greater the potential for growth. The shorter the investment timeframe, the greater the risk of loss. Remember, though, that investing in the stock market continues to outpace other forms of investing.

Deciding When to Sell a Stock

Most investors don't even think about selling their stocks; figuring out what to buy and when to buy it is the hard part. But at some point you will probably have to consider selling, for a variety of reasons:

❖ The stock that you bought isn't performing well, and you don't see any prospects for improvement.

❖ The stock that you bought has performed extremely well, and it now represents too much of your portfolio (remember, you don't want too many eggs in one basket).

❖ You need cash to make a different investment (either another stock or possibly a bond).

❖ The stock doesn't meet your criteria any longer (for example, the growth rate is too low, the P/E ratio is too high, and so on).

❖ The company has had a change in management or corporate philosophy to a team or point of view that you don't agree with.

❖ You need cash for an immediate expense.

Adopt a discipline for selling, and stick to it. Know what criteria will have to be met for you to sell. It sounds a bit crazy to be ready to dump a stock the instant you buy it, but if you have those requirements in mind at the beginning, you will be much less likely to be stuck with something that doesn't meet your needs.

Whatever the reason, you can't expect to hold a stock forever. Go back to that wardrobe analogy for a minute. Your clothes wear out. They go out of fashion. You gain or lose weight, and they don't fit anymore. You retire and just don't need those work clothes. If you never cleaned out your closet, you would have a roomful of smocked dresses from fourth grade. Think of your stocks the same way. At some point, they just may not fit your needs anymore. When that happens, you need to consider selling. You don't want a portfolio full of the wrong stocks because you were unwilling or unable to sell those that just didn't fit the bill any longer.

Now you know how to invest in stocks. Next, I'll teach you how to invest in bonds.

The Bottom Line

Investing in stocks is not difficult. Women like you across the country are trading stock right now.

Reader's Journal:

Knowledge Gained:

_____
_____
_____
_____
_____
_____
_____
_____
_____
_____

Steps I Will Take:

_____
_____
_____
_____
_____
_____
_____
_____
_____
_____

Mrs. Ladden, a widow in her 70s, sat down in the chair and showed me her statement. "Mrs. Owens, I don't want to talk with any of those young financial consultants. Here's my bank statement. I have three certificates of deposit that will mature tomorrow, and the interest rate that my bank quoted me is far below what my CDs have been earning. I use the interest to supplement my income, and I can't afford to take a pay cut. I need to earn more money, but I can't take a lot of risk. Can you show me what my options are?"

At this stage in my career, I was a branch manager vice president of an investment center in Washington, D.C. Ideally, I did not sit down with clients and discuss investment strategy. My heart, not my head, took over. I could see the concern in her eyes.

We hunkered down in my office, and I reviewed all of her statements to get a clearer picture of her situation. Mrs. Ladden had been investing in certificates of deposit at her bank since her husband died 10 years ago. Her husband had handled all of their finances, and upon his death she took on the responsibility. However, 10 years ago she had been earning upward of 10 percent annually on her CDs. Current interest rates were now half of what they used to be, and her income was declining.

Although the home she lived in was paid for, property taxes and utilities continued to increase. She was worried that she would outlive her money. Her biggest fear was losing her principal. I knew that whether she realized it or not, she was already taking a risk with her money. If interest rates continued to fall, she would not be able to keep up with inflation. Clearly, her objective was to achieve an increase in income without taking on more risk.

Together, we decided on a strategy. First, she invested in Treasury bonds that matured in 5 to 10 years. Eventually, she shifted some money into corporate bonds that paid her a higher interest rate. The process was arduous at first, but once she understood what her different income options were, she was able to make good choices. Her portfolio expanded to include different types of bonds that matured at different times. It wasn't long before she was able to look at a weekly bond offering list and call in to place an order on her own.

Chapter 9

How to Invest in Bonds

The Bottom Line

Bonds may not be as glamorous or exciting as stocks, but if you need income they are an essential ingredient in your investment portfolio.

Pick up a newspaper, turn to the financial page, and scan the columns for the word *bonds*. It may not be there. There are pages and pages of stocks and mutual funds listed, plus some other stock-related categories, but bonds, if they are listed at all, don't get equal billing. Yet bonds could be a very important part of your portfolio.

Bonds are the quiet sidekicks of stocks, putting out steady streams of income while stocks spurt and tank their way up—and sometimes down—the charts. Not that bonds never go down. They do, but only rarely.

Bonds do some very nice things for investors. I want you to get to know them, and in the course of assembling your investment products into your portfolio, include bonds.

As with stocks, you need to choose how you want to own bonds: in a self-directed account, with input from an adviser; with a private portfolio manager; or in a mutual fund.

As a bondholder, you are a *creditor* of a company. This means that instead of owing the company money, the company owes you money because you're extending it credit. Bonds are typically sold at *face* or *par value* of $1,000. The issuing company has borrowed money from you for a defined period of time or *term* and is paying you a fixed rate of interest for the use of your money. At the end of the term, the bond *matures*, and your original investment is returned to you.

Many people use bond interest to supplement their income; thus, people invest in bonds when they need income right away, rather than wait until later to receive it as with stocks.

Bondholders don't participate in the gain or loss in value of a company in the way that stockholders do. Bondholders are paid interest known as the *coupon rate* or *nominal yield*. If bonds are held to *maturity*, there is no gain or loss on the investment.

Bonds are considered a conservative investment and are more secure than stocks. In the event of *bankruptcy,* all creditors and bondholders are paid in full before stockholders receive any return of their investment.

However, it's important to realize that bonds do fluctuate in value in response to changes in interest rates in the economy. As interest rates in the economy rise, the price of bonds declines. As interest rates in the economy decline, the price of bonds rises.

The Appeal of Bonds

As the preceding sidebar describes, stocks represent ownership in a company, and bonds represent a creditor relationship with a company. If you own a bond issued by XYZ Company, then XYZ owes you a debt.

Bonds are certainly not very glamorous, especially when compared to stocks. But investors find them appealing because of their more staid personality. What do bonds do for a portfolio? They provide three things: income, safety of principal, and diversification.

Coaching Tip

Bonds are called fixed income investments because the interest on the bond never varies. If a bond pays 6 percent, it always pays 6 percent.

Income

How much income do bonds provide? Well, bonds yielded or gave more than three times their current returns than stocks did over the 10 years that ended December 31, 1997. At the same time, bonds were three times less volatile than stocks. Remember, with bonds you are paid interest every six months. This interest income is your current return or yield.

How much of your return comes from income? Take a look at the following chart. Most of your return comes from income in the case of bonds, whereas with stocks the opposite is true. Most of you return comes from the appreciation or increase of value of your stock.

	Price Appreciation	Income
Bonds	9%	91%
Stocks	69%	31%

Safety of Principal

Of course, safety of principal depends on the issuer's credit strength, but as a bondholder, you can have a reasonable expectation that your principal, the face amount of the bond, will be paid back to you in full on the maturity date. If you sell the bond before maturity, though, you take your chances that the market price of the bond may be more or less than what you paid.

Diversification

Diversification comes from the fact that stocks and bonds usually behave differently at any given time. The idea is that when your stocks aren't performing well, your bonds hopefully will be, and vice versa.

Two Primary Characteristics of Bonds

These three benefits of bonds come from two primary characteristics: a set interest rate and a maturity date. Because of the set interest rate, bonds are often called "fixed-income securities." You know what you'll get before you get it. This is good for the budget, especially when you're on a fixed income.

Typically, bonds make their interest payments to bondholders every six months. Mrs. Ladden built her budget around these interest payments. The maturity date, as stated earlier, is the date when you as the bondholder get back the face amount of the bond. You loan the company money, it pays you interest for loaning it, and then you get your money back.

Many years ago, bonds were issued in paper form with small coupons attached to the bottom. Bondholders would spend a great deal of time clipping the coupons and turning them in to the bank to receive their interest payments. Now, many bonds are issued in "book entry only" form. This means that no paper bond will ever be issued, and the bond must be held in a brokerage account. The investment company is then responsible for collecting your interest payments from the issuer and crediting them to your account at their company.

A convertible bond has all of the characteristics of a bond, with a twist! It is convertible to common stock at the discretion of the bondholder.

Convertible bonds typically pay a slightly lower rate of interest than a non-convertible bond. The bondholder accepts a lower rate of interest for the advantage of being able to convert the bond to a stock holding.

A Company's Credit Rating

To give investors an idea of how reliable a bond may be, several firms issue credit ratings on corporate debt. The most-used reference sources are *Moody's* and *Standard & Poor*. Their ratings are broken down into six basic categories.

	Standard & Poor	Moody's
Investment grade	AAA	Aaa
	AA	Aa
	A	A
	BBB	Baa
	BB	Ba
Below investment grade	B	B

Just as a bank chooses whom to lend money to based on credit history, you will, in part, choose which bonds to own based on the company's credit rating.

Bonds are issued for a fixed period of time and have a known "maturity date." Some bonds are sold with the stipulation that the company can "call" them before maturity. Typically, though, bonds are issued with a period of "call protection," a period of time when the issuer is not able to "call" the bonds.

As a bondholder, a call feature is usually undesirable because there is a chance that the bond will be paid off before maturity. To offset this feature, callable bonds typically pay a slightly higher rate of interest than a non-callable bond issued by the same or similarly rated company. At first blush, this doesn't seem to be such a bad thing, but let's look at this call feature carefully.

Why would a company want to include a call feature in a bond? If a bond is issued with a fixed rate of 8 percent, you can assume that it is a competitive interest rate on the date that the bond is issued. If it is a 20-year bond, this means that the company will pay $80 per year for each $1,000 bond issued for 20 years. If the company had $500,000 in outstanding bonds, the company would be required to pay $40,000 in interest per year, or total interest payments over the life of the bond of $800,000.

What if interest rates declined to 6 percent a year after the bond is issued? Wouldn't it make sense for the company to call the 8 percent bond, pay off these bondholders, and then issue a 6 percent 19-year bond? You bet it would!

The company could save $190,000 in interest expense by calling these bonds and reissuing them at 6 percent for the balance of the term. That's why issuers frequently include a call feature in a bond issue.

Default Risk

With any bond, there is a possibility that the issuer will fail to pay off the bond at maturity. In other words, the company might not be able to pay you back. This is default risk and is precisely why many people pay close attention to an issuer's credit rating. In exchange for increased risk of default, a company, or issuer, will increase the amount of interest that it pays to make its bond more attractive and make up for its higher risk factors.

Interest Rates and Bond Prices

The company that issues a bond will always pay interest at the coupon rate. Because that coupon rate is fixed, a bond's price will move up and down to make the bond's yield more closely reflect current interest rates. It's very much like a teeter-totter. If interest rates go up, the bond's price goes down. If interest rates go down, the bond's price goes up.

For instance, let's look at a bond with one year left until maturity and a 5 percent coupon rate. At maturity, this bond will return $1,000. If the interest rate for one-year bonds is 5 percent, then the bond will trade at "par," or 100. That means that the price of the bond is 100 percent of face value. If the interest rate for one-year bonds moves to 6 percent, then the bond will trade at a "discount," or less than 100. If interest rates for that maturity drop to 4 percent, then the bond will trade at a "premium," or more than 100.

Current interest rate	4%	5%	6%
Face value	1,000	1,000	1,000
Coupon	5%	5%	5%
Current price	125.00	100.00	83.33
Current yield	$50/$1,250 = 4%	$50/$1,000 = 5%	$50/$833 = 6%

Notice that the current yield and the current interest rates are the same.

Let's work through an example:

ABC Utility Corporation

Purchase price: 99.000

Coupon rate: 5.0%

Current yield: 5.05%

Maturity date: January 1, 2010

If you buy $10,000 face value of the ABC bond, then you will receive $10,000 back on January 1, 2010. To buy the bond, you pay 99 percent of the face value, or $9,900 ($10,000 × 99.000% = $9,900).

Remember, the bond pays interest every six months—in this case, on January 1 and July 1 each year until maturity. So, if you buy the bond between these two coupon payment dates, you also pay a prorated amount of interest. However, when the next coupon payment is made, and you own the bond at that time, you keep the entire coupon payment.

Who Issues Bonds?

Generally, bonds are issued by one of three types of entities: corporations, the federal government and its agencies, or state governments and their political subdivisions.

Interest paid by corporate bonds is always taxable. However, the federal and state governments engage in a reciprocal deal. The federal government promises not to tax state bond income, and the state governments promise not to tax federal bond income. Therefore, interest on Treasury bills, notes, and bonds are federally income taxable but are not taxed by the states. State bonds, on the other hand, are exempt from federal income taxes.

When a bond is called, the issuer returns the principal to the bondholder. At first blush, this doesn't sound too bad, but let's look at it from the investor's point of view.

Because bondholders are typically seeking a steady stream of income from their bonds, getting their principal back when interest rates are down is not necessarily a good thing.

Instead of holding an investment that will consistently pay 8 percent over the course of 20 years, the principal is returned to the investor prematurely. When the bondholder is paid in full, the company stops making interest payments to the bondholder. The investor is left in the position of needing to find another income-producing investment at a time when competitive interest rates for similarly rated bonds are just 6 percent. The bondholder's income has decreased, through no fault of her own. The bondholder is not happy. This is what is known as *reinvestment risk*, the risk that the investor will be forced to reinvest during a time when conditions are less ideal to the investor.

The Yield Curve

Normally, the longer the maturity on a bond is, the higher the interest rate paid. The increase is fairly pronounced at first and then levels off as the length of the bond increases. Occasionally, unique economic circumstances create an "inverted yield curve." This is where interest rates actually decline the longer the term of the bond is. An explanation of why this happens would easily take up several chapters in a basic economics textbook. But you should know that this is an unusual event, and it will eventually revert back to a normal yield curve.

Interest Rate Risk

Interest rate risk runs in two directions:

1. The possibility that interest rates will rise, causing a bond to decrease in price at the time that an investor needs to sell that bond. This environment will likely cause a capital loss upon the sale of a bond.

2. The possibility that interest rates will fall at the time that a bond matures, leaving the investor to reinvest in another bond at a lower interest rate. This environment will produce a lower income stream from the same amount of invested funds.

Coaching Tip

Junk bonds are high-yield bonds. They are not investment grade. A certain percentage of your bond allocation could easily be in high-yield bonds. This gives you the potential for higher interest.

Bond Insurance

Several companies offer insurance to bond issuers. Any bond that is insured is automatically rated "AAA." However, keep in mind that this insurance guarantees only that the bond will make its interest payments on time and that it will pay the face amount upon maturity. Insurance does not guarantee that an investor will make money on a bond.

Remember, as interest rates move, the price of bonds moves. A bond investor may experience negative returns precisely because of those price fluctuations.

The Bottom Line

Bonds give you income to count on and are an effective hedge, or protection, against your stock investments.

Reader's Journal:

Knowledge Gained:

_____

_____

_____

_____

_____

_____

_____

_____

_____

_____

Steps I Will Take:

_____

_____

_____

_____

_____

_____

_____

_____

_____

_____

Ann wanted to give her 17-year-old daughter, Sybil, something for her birthday that would last a lifetime, so she bought two hours of my time to meet about investing.

At our first meeting, Sybil and I talked about her interests and ambitions. She had many. One was law school, an ambition that would definitely require money. Knowing that we would be talking, Sybil had already talked with her friends about what companies to invest in. Like most teenagers, she had a keen interest in food and clothes. As a result, she thought she might want to invest in The Gap clothing store or Krispy Kreme donuts.

I assigned Sybil homework in preparation for our next session. First, I asked her to read a book that I gave her about teens and investing. Next, I asked her to visit a library to research information about The Gap and Krispy Kreme. She left eager to do both the reading and the research.

(By the way, Sybil's mother was willing to match Sybil's investment each month if Sybil would invest a portion of her allowance. This mother was doing a brilliant job of paving the way for her daughter's financial success.)

At our second session, Sybil came prepared. Based on her own research, she had changed her mind about investing in The Gap and Krispy Kreme, not because they were poor choices, but because they were currently trading at their highest levels for the year. She also noticed that her friends had stopped buying from one of the stores.

Sybil told me that based on her findings, she would rather invest in a mutual fund because she could get diversification and have her money managed by a professional money manager. I was impressed.

We turned on the computer and visited some Web sites that could help Sybil narrow her choice of mutual funds. She ultimately chose an aggressive growth fund that would allow her to invest the additional amounts monthly, matched by her mother's contribution. Directly off the Internet, we were able to print out an application and prospectus (see the samples in this chapter) and mail off a check to the investment company that evening.

In just a short time of study, Sybil was able to make a competent choice for herself. Like you, she is on her way to a life of investing, which means a life with the kind of financial support that she needs to thrive.

Chapter 10

How to Invest in Mutual Funds

The Bottom Line

Mutual funds are an excellent investment product for busy people
who want to own an assortment of stock managed by a professional.

The party is on when it comes to investing in mutual funds!
Mutual funds have become tremendously popular for several reasons:

1. They enable you to invest with others, so your money goes
   farther, in a sense.
2. The funds are affordable.
3. You can choose from more than 7,500 funds.
4. The 7,500 funds are versatile, giving you a wide range of
   choices.

5. Funds give you built-in diversification, an assortment of stocks and sometimes bonds, so all of your money isn't in one stock or bond.

6. Funds are managed by managers that you can read up on to learn their style and record.

7. They fit into a busy person's life.

8. They are simple to purchase.

9. You can track mutual funds in the same way that you track stocks and bonds—in the newspaper, on television, on the radio, and, of course, via the Internet.

How Mutual Funds Work

Let's say that you and nine friends decide to create a mutual fund. You each put up $1,000, so you have a total of $10,000 to invest. You find someone to manage the money for the group, and she invests in 10 different stocks. A year later, the total value of your funds increases to $12,000. The value of your share of the fund is now $12,000, or $\frac{1}{10}$ of the total value.

This is how you invest in mutual funds, except that you aren't investing with a circle of friends—you're investing with people you have probably never met. Your money is being pooled for mutual benefit.

Jody Temple-White, a financial planner and co-founder of The Everywoman's Company, spins off the idea of pooling money by using her local swim park to illustrate how a mutual fund works. I like it—it makes sense. See what you think.

Swim parks have a diverse set of pools under one roof—a family of pools, so to speak. This is like a family of mutual funds, diverse yet under the roof of one company.

There are two ways to get into a swim park: pay for getting in on that day, or pay a flat fee for an unlimited number of visits to the swim park for a year. This is similar to paying to get into many mutual funds. You pay a front-end sales charge to put your money in a fund, but once that money is in the account, most funds will let you move from fund to fund without paying more. (There are other ways to pay sales charges for mutual funds, outlined elsewhere in this chapter.)

The pools in the swim park vary in depth and risk, from the infant pool to the lap pool, to the wave simulation pool, to the diving pool. Think of these pools as funds. Each has its own purpose, so to speak. The infant pool would not be appropriate for a 12-year-old who loves to dive.

Each of these pools has a lifeguard to watch over it. The lifeguard watches every aspect of the pool, from the swimmers and safety to the quality of the water. The lifeguard is in charge of who enters the pool and who exits the pool, and their behavior while there. Think of the lifeguard as the money manager of your mutual fund.

If you swim in the lap pool, you're there to swim the distance, just as you would in a growth mutual fund. The pool is designed for distance, not for leisure, and while you can get in and out of the lap pool at will, there are no steps on the side to make it easy. In a similar way, you can get out of growth funds early, but it takes some effort and sometimes costs you money.

The wave pools at the center are for stronger swimmers who can absorb the undertow, as in an aggressive mutual fund in which you have lots of ups and downs, like the waves.

The shallow pool lets you get used to the water without diving in. This is like bonds, or income funds.

The hot tub at the swim center is a place to park your body between pools, to give yourself a rest. This is similar to money market funds, where you park your money while you decide what to do with it next.

There you go. Now even your swim center will remind you to invest!

Researching Mutual Funds

Sybil went to the library and found what she needed to know about growth mutual funds. She was headed for law school and wanted to purchase a home shortly after graduation. That gave her a bit more than seven years to invest.

We also used the Internet and found www.quicken.com particularly helpful. Quicken has a mutual fund finder tool that provides you with suggestions based on the criteria that you enter. Your criteria will be your set of answers to questions like these:

1. Do you want your money to grow over time? How long?
2. Do you want your money to produce income right away?
3. Do you want your money to bring both growth and income?
4. Do you want to put your money in a place where it grows yet gives you quick access to it?
5. How aggressive or cautious do you need to be?

6. Do you have a special interest in international or socially responsible funds, or in a specific sector like technology?

7. How many years have you been investing?

8. How old are you?

9. What is your net worth?

Sybil and I narrowed our selection to the top 25 growth mutual funds over 10 years. From that list, we were able to eliminate quite a few because many were sector funds. Remember, sector funds invest your money in one industry rather than several, although they are diverse within that sector. Sybil had decided, and I agreed, that she wanted diversification, or stocks from a number of companies in various industries.

If you go to the Quicken site, or another one that provides a similar screening, and you print out a list of funds that match your criteria. You can then look the funds up in the "Morningstar Mutual Fund Guide," in print or online. Remember, Morningstar is considered the Bible of mutual fund ratings and is the most frequently quoted. Look up each fund, and mark the ones that still appeal to you.

 Coaching Tip

You can look, but don't react. I don't think you are a more successful investor if you have instant information. It may be just the opposite.

Other helpful research tools, in addition to Morningstar, are listed here:

1. **Value Line**—Provides research and ranking on mutual funds as well as stocks.

2. **Lipper Analytical**—Provides the most extensive of all research and analysis for mutual funds to financial and investment companies. This information is used on sites such as www.cbsmarketwatch.com, www.kiplinger.com, and www.thestreet.com.

I like the Financial Engines site, at www.financialengines.com. It analyzes your portfolio, compares it to your goals, and lets you know if you're going to make it. The mind behind www.financialengines.com is William Sharp, who was awarded the Nobel Prize in Economics for his Modern Portfolio theory. There is a small fee attached to the service, but I think it's worth it. Here's how it works:

1. You go to the site and enter the investment products in your portfolio and your goals. For example, your current portfolio is invested in several mutual funds and you want to retire in 12 years at 57.

2. Financial Engines analyzes your portfolio and your goals, and then prints out how close you'll come with your current investment products. It then makes recommendations on specific adjustments that you can make to reach your goals, or to at least get you closer to them.

Coaching Tip

When you know how much is enough, you can manage your money so you have enough.

Types of Funds

There are currently more than 7,500 different mutual funds. Of those, 4,600 are growth funds, or funds investing in a variety of stocks. Imagine how Sybil felt. She went from having an idea of investing in two stocks to discovering more than 4,000 choices that could meet her needs.

It's actually quite easy—even fun—to make your selection of mutual funds, because your choice will be a result of answers to the preceding questions. Clarity surfaces when you know what you want.

The 7,500 funds can really be boiled down to four types:

1. **Stock mutual funds (growth funds)**—When you want your money to grow

2. **Bond mutual funds (income funds)**—When you want income now

3. **Hybrid mutual funds (growth and income)**—When you want both growth and income

4. **Money market funds**—When you want a place to park your money for the short term or as a savings account

By the way, there are many other variations of mutual funds that may or may not ever interest you.

Money market funds are often misunderstood, and you'll want to have a clear picture of their usefulness.

Money market funds are often confused with money market accounts. There are differences, as the following table shows.

Money Market Funds	Money Market Accounts
Issued by a mutual fund company	Issued by a bank or credit union
Not insured by FDIC (but seldom, if ever, has needed to be insured)	Insured by FDIC
Perceived as difficult to get to money (not necessarily true)	Perceived as easy to get to your your money (not necessarily true)
Usually unlimited free access	Often restricted free access
Earns a percentage on your money	Earns a percentage on your money

As you can see, money market funds and money market accounts are quite similar; their interest rates also are often very competitive. Investors often use money market funds to park their money while they wait to buy a particular fund or decide what fund they want to buy. For example, if you wanted to buy a Fidelity mutual fund but weren't sure which one you were going to select, you might want to invest in a Fidelity money market fund. Then, when you select the Fidelity mutual fund you want, you could move your money from the money market fund into the mutual fund at no cost.

If you're building your three- or six-month emergency savings, or if you're saving for something that you will buy in less than a year, a money market fund or account will work for you. If you're stacking your money while waiting to buy a mutual fund, a money market fund will serve you well. But both work—go for the best rate and terms.

Within the four types of mutual funds (stock, bond, hybrid, and money market) there are varieties of funds that focus on specific areas and that are managed in different styles. Let's take a look at the different types of stock funds you could invest in.

Types	Companies
Aggressive growth	Small, emerging companies
Growth	Large- and mid-cap companies
Growth and income	Large, dividend-paying companies
Sector funds	Industry-specific companies
International funds	International companies

Different-sized companies issue stocks; as a result, mutual funds are created that invest based on the market capitalization of those companies—that is, their classification as small caps, medium caps, and large caps. Investing in funds that specialize in only one of these caps can increase risk because all the stock in those funds could be affected at the same time by a business or economic cycle.

This brings us to another kind of fund: the sector fund. In Chapter 8, "How to Invest in Stocks," we discussed the 10 major industry classifications. There are "sector funds" that invest in stocks in these industries and focus even more narrowly. For example, the computer industry has spawned several sector funds under its category:

Types	Examples
Technology funds	T. Rowe Price Science and Technology
Software funds	Fidelity Select Software
E-commerce funds	Etrade Ecommerce Fund
Internet funds	Munder NetNet Fund
Networking funds	Fidelity Networking and Infrastructure

As you become more confident in your investing ability, you will learn a lot about yourself. One thing you'll learn is how often you need to check on your investments. How often will you take a look at how your money is doing?

Some investors, men as often as women, put their money into a fund and allow themselves to check on it only twice a year. Why? If they look at where their investments are every day, they could get nervous, even obsessed. They've learned that they're better off not looking and have built boundaries that keep them focused on other important parts of their lives.

At the other end of investment behaviors are investors who enjoy keeping in touch with how their money—even their long-term money—is doing. They might keep a network such as CNBC on mute in their office all day just so they can look up and see the ticker running along the bottom of the screen. These people have probably also signed up for a reporting service to alert them to changes in their portfolio, or their set of investment products. The alert comes to them over their mobile phones or wireless assistants. These investors not only look, but they look continually.

Which type of looker are you?

Track the Funds

Initially, mutual funds come to market at $10 a share and are seeded or started with money from the mutual fund company. The price of a share is called the "net asset value," or "NAV." The NAV is calculated by totaling the value of all the stocks and bonds in a fund at the end of the trading day, and dividing it by the number of shares of the fund that are outstanding. When you look in the newspaper for your fund's NAV, you will notice that it also tells you how much your fund's price changed from the previous day.

You may already read the financial page of the newspaper. If you don't, start now. Go grab the paper. Turn to the financial section, and familiarize yourself with your newspaper's stock market and mutual fund pages. Or, subscribe to *The Wall Street Journal* or *Barron's,* two excellent ways to learn. Spend time there exploring, making yourself comfortable in the world of money—your money.

Here's a simple way to measure your risk tolerance. It will also help you know your selling point if an investment ever goes down.

Ask yourself this: If I had $10,000 to invest and my growth investment was performing the same as every other growth investment and they were all going down, at what point would I sell? At what point would I start losing sleep over the investment?

See what type of risk-taker you are, based on your answer:

- ❖ **$9,000**—Your sleep quotient is 10 percent. You have a low risk tolerance.
- ❖ **$5,000**—Your sleep quotient is 50 percent. You are very risk tolerant.
- ❖ **$1,000**—You're a gambler and probably lose sleep when you're *not* investing.

Important note: If your growth fund is tanking, or going down without sign of reviving, when other funds are going up, sell it, unless you have a very good reason to think that it will climb back.

Must Reading: The Prospectus

By law, all mutual funds must state the type of securities that the fund manager will invest in. Potential investors read it and are able to determine whether the fund is a fit for them, based on its stated objective. The document is called a prospectus. Prospectuses are famous for being long and difficult reading. Because there are more investors than ever before, and because the competition greater, some mutual fund companies are making an effort to create a readable prospectus.

Every prospectus must be submitted to the Securities and Exchange Commission (SEC) for approval. However, the SEC does *not* endorse any investment product. It simply works to ensure that the prospectus meets all the legal requirements in place. The prospectus offers essential information about the mutual fund. It not only details the objective of the fund, it also gives the fund manager's resumé, expenses, fees, performance history, and a number of other helpful facts, including the style that the manager will use when buying securities.

The sole purpose of the prospectus is to make sure that you understand the cost and risks of investing in the mutual fund. You must receive a prospectus to make an investment. Because a prospectus can make for difficult reading, the SEC has recently begun to require companies to create a more reader-friendly introductory section. Use it as your starting point, and read it to get an initial overview and sense about the fund. Then read the rest of it to find out answers to specific questions that you may have about a fund.

Two important sections of the prospectus to read are "Fees" and "Performance." This will inform you about what you will pay to invest in your mutual fund and will educate you about what performance you can expect to receive from the fund.

A Fund's Fees

Before you invest in a mutual fund, you need to know what it will cost you from the time you first invest to the time you sell. Mutual fund companies, and fund managers, do not work for free; nor should they. As a consumer, it's your responsibility to know what you are paying for their services so that you can make an educated decision about what fund to select.

Several fees are associated with mutual funds, and it's important to understand what those fees are and how you pay them. In addition, any fund also has trading expenses (which will vary depending on how much the portfolio is traded or turned over) and advertising costs. Those expenses are all subtracted from the fund's net asset value (NAV), or share price.

As a fund owner, you won't see those costs itemized on your statement. You will have to read the prospectus in great detail to find the amount of the management fee. But because they are variable costs, the advertising and trading expenses are reported only after the fact in a fund's annual report.

There are no-load funds and load funds. "Load" simply means sales charge. So, a load fund comes with a sales charge, and a no-load fund comes without one. The sales charge is the commission; it compensates the adviser for her services. Make no mistake: Regardless of what type of fund you own, all funds—both load and no-load—charge you in some way for management fees, trading costs, and advertising expenses.

I like to use a turnpike analogy when describing how fees are charged and paid for. You're on the East Coast driving west on a turnpike called The Mutual Fund. Like any turnpike, there are tollbooths. After all, it's the turnpike that's making it possible for you to drive across the country.

When you enter the turnpike, you don't know if you want to drive the entire way or if you want to take some side trips. You have four choices on how to pay your way:

1. You can pay the full amount by purchasing a pass that you can use along the way. These are called "A shares."

2. You can get on without paying anything, but if you decide to get off before the end of the turnpike, you pay a toll. These are called "B shares."

3. You don't pay anything to get on the turnpike, but you will pay something to get off. The amount depends upon how far west you go before exiting. Your fee will be less if you get off in Montana than if you get off in Pennsylvania. These are called "C shares."

4. You don't pay to get on the turnpike, and you put in a token at tollbooths along the way, getting on and off any exit you please. These are called "no loads."

You can pay for a mutual fund at three times: when you buy it, while you own it, and when you sell it. Take a look at the following table.

Type of Fund	Sales Charge to Buy	Sales Charge to Own	Sales Charge to Sell
A shares	Yes	Lower expenses	No
B shares	No	Midrange expenses	Maybe (required holding period of four to seven years)
C shares	No	Higher expenses	No (if held for one year)
No-load shares	No	Varies	No

How much are these sales charges? For specific information on an individual fund, you must refer to that fund's prospectus. To give you a general idea, A shares usually cost around 6 percent up front. The more money you place with a particular fund family, the lower the up-front cost of the A shares. These percentages drop at specific dollar amounts called breakpoints. Read your prospectus to find out where those breakpoints are. Generally speaking, if you put $1 million or more into a single fund family, the entire load on your A share will be waived.

B shares charge a "contingent deferred sales charge" (CDSC). In our example, these are charged if you come off the road early. This means that instead of charging you to buy the fund, the fund family wants a commitment from you as a shareholder to stay within the family for a certain period of time. This can be as few as four years or as many as eight. If you sell and get out of the fund family before the required time has passed, you will be charged a fee. The longer you've been in, the lower the fee will be.

C shares have a required holding period of only one year. If you sell before the year is up, the charge is only around 1 percent.

Coaching Tip

If you don't want to pay for advice, you can do it yourself. If you are educated about investing and know what you want, you can likely do a good job. It takes time, interest, and skill.

The type of fee you're charged will be determined by the process that you use to invest. As an adviser, I was paid an hourly fee, and Sybil invested in a no-load mutual fund. If you're reading this book and decide to do the research on your own, you won't have to pay that fee. If you use an investment adviser, you might purchase A, B, C, or no-load shares, depending upon how the adviser is compensated. (We discuss how advisers are paid in Chapter 17, "Selecting Your Best Advisers.")

A Fund's Performance

You judge how your funds are performing based on how much the value of your investment increased over what you invested. When Sybil and I conducted research, we used the mutual fund's past performance as one of our criteria. However, when you see the fund's average annual return quoted in the paper or in an advertisement, recognize that performance is based on a certain time period. Not all investors earned that return because not everyone purchased on December 31 of the prior year, or whatever date the return represents. Here's how you can calculate a fund's actual return.

$$\frac{\text{Current value} - \text{original investment}}{\text{original investment}}$$

The amount of time that you have held your investment in the fund will allow you to determine the annual return. If you want to know how much you earned per year, divide the overall return by the number of years.

If you want to measure how an investment has performed over longer periods of time, calculate the fund's average annual return, or AAR. Most funds do better some years than others. To give investors a sense of what the performance is over time, fund companies average the level of performance by dividing performance by the number of years that the fund has been in existence.

A Manager's Style

Fund managers also define their mutual funds by one of three investment styles:

❖ **Growth.** These managers look primarily at growth, trying to find stocks that are growing faster than their competitors, or faster than the market as a whole. These funds buy shares in companies that are growing rapidly—often well-known, established corporations.

❖ **Value.** These fund managers use a value approach to stocks, searching for stocks that are undervalued when compared to other, similar companies. Often the share prices of these stocks have been beaten down by the market as investors have become pessimistic about the potential of these companies.

❖ **Blends, or blend approach.** These fund managers buy both kinds of stocks, building a portfolio of both growth and value stocks.

Make Your Choice

You've done the research. Now it's time to select your mutual fund. Your selection requires the same steps and answers as any investment decision. Let's use Sybil's situation as an example:

1. **Investment objective:** *What do you want the money to do?* Answer: Sybil wanted the money to pay for law school and to use as a down payment on a house after graduation.

2. **Time frame:** *How long before you want to use the money?* Answer: Sybil had seven to eight years.

3. **Risk:** *How much risk are you willing to take?* Answer: Sybil had a high risk preference.

Sybil examined the remaining mutual funds on her list. She made her choice based on her answers, her research, and her instincts. Right there in front of the computer, we printed out an application and sent the check. At 17, Sybil was an investor—and an educated one.

Coaching Tip

The investment objective of the fund should match your investment objective. This is the first place you look when selecting a mutual fund. Make sure it meets your objectives.

Dollar Cost Averaging

As you make plans to invest in mutual funds, you need to know about dollar cost averaging, a simple, automatic, and potentially profitable way for you to invest.

Most mutual funds and investment firms have programs available for you to "dollar cost average." Dollar cost averaging is the process by which you invest a specific amount of money on a set schedule, regardless of what the market is doing. This works to your benefit because you're making disciplined investments—half the battle for most people. Dollar cost averaging is also beneficial because it enables you to automatically buy more shares when the price is lower and then to buy fewer shares when the price is higher. You don't have to have a lot of money to invest this way. Some fund families offer this service for as little as $25 a month. All you have to do is fill out a couple of forms and provide a voided check or deposit slip.

Dollar Cost Averaging

Month	Monthly Amount	Price of Shares	# of Shares Purchased	Ending Value
January	$100.00	$10.00	10	$100.00
February	$100.00	$9.50	10.53	$195.00
March	$100.00	$9.00	11.11	$351.50
April	$100.00	$8.25	12.12	$361.50
May	$100.00	$9.50	10.53	$517.80
June	$100.00	$9.75	10.26	$629.40
Totals	$600.00	$9.33 AVG	61.30	$629.40

By purchasing shares systematically, you reduce your chances of buying shares at their highest levels. It averages out your cost per share.

Stay Involved

It's easy to become passive when investing in mutual funds. Most of the investing decisions are made by the investment company and the fund manager. But stay involved. Check in. Review and evaluate the performance of your investments and the fund manager. If you're using an adviser, schedule a checkup every six months. If you're investing on your own, take the time to review the statements that you receive from the investment company quarterly.

Compare your fund's performance to the indexes that represent it. For example, if you're invested in an aggressive growth fund with small companies, you would want to know how the Russell 2000 Index (an index consisting of small company stocks) has performed over the same time frame. Should you change if it's underperforming? That's your call, with the help of your adviser or investment club.

You are ultimately responsible for the care of your portfolio. You created it, and it's yours to grow.

The Bottom Line

Mutual funds offer you a lot of interesting choices and convenience as an investor.

Reader's Journal:

Knowledge Gained:

_____

_____

_____

_____

_____

_____

_____

_____

_____

Steps I Will Take:

_____

_____

_____

_____

_____

_____

_____

_____

_____

_____

Kasey's first investment other than her retirement plan at work was a mutual fund recommended by the representative who administered her 403(b) plan. She went on to open a discount brokerage account to buy a specific stock that interested her.

Kasey had attended a women's networking event and was impressed by the guest speaker, who had given a presentation on women and investing. Soon afterward, she called to make an appointment with the speaker and ultimately transferred her brokerage account to the speaker's firm to benefit from the research and recommendations that the firm offered.

As the relationship between Kasey and her adviser grew, Kasey relied on her for education in the financial markets and for investment recommendations. Her assets increased, she started her own business, and Kasey had new concerns. How could she reduce her taxes? How could she defer more income from the business she had started?

Kasey's needs were changing, and she wanted more expertise in her areas of concern. It was time for her to start making longer-term plans, and she wanted to put together a financial road map that she could use to reach her goals.

Kasey asked other investors who they used as an adviser. She chose several to interview and selected someone she felt would help her play at a new level.

Looking back over her financial path, Kasey realized that each time her needs changed, she developed a new financial relationship.

At each stage of the development of Kasey's portfolio, she adjusted her investment choices. Her success began with a $50-a-month mutual fund investment; it now tops six figures.

Chapter 11

Where to Invest

The Bottom Line

Where you shop for financial services depends on what type of help you want. This is not a one-size-fits-all model.

There are more than 5,500 securities firms, with 82,000 branch offices across the United States. It can be a real challenge to determine where to invest your money. Each of these firms employs financial services professionals who specialize in certain products or services.

Kasey's experience is pretty typical for most investors. Our needs dictate what types of services we choose. Kasey's first investment in a mutual fund worked because, at the time, she wanted convenience.

Investment or Mutual Fund Companies

The gentleman who helped Kasey initially was a representative of the investment company that administered her employer's retirement plan. Investment companies, or mutual fund companies, market mutual funds and administer retirement plans for employers. These types of plans are one of the first investments that the average person makes.

Those who help you invest in your plans and mutual funds are usually "registered representatives" of large mutual fund conglomerates. These representatives are licensed and don't make specific recommendations. They assist people who are comfortable deciding what they want to invest in.

Many of these companies have several mutual funds available to you to invest in on your own, outside of your employer's retirement or stock plans. You can open an account by sending for an application and prospectus in the mail or by accessing these forms on the mutual fund company's Web site. Many of the large mutual fund companies, such as those listed here, now offer a menu of services such as discount brokerage.

According to *Money* magazine, these are the largest mutual fund companies:

Fidelity Investments

Vanguard

American Funds

Putnam

Janus

Franklin Funds

Aim

T. Rowe Price

American Century

MFS Funds

When Kasey decided to invest an extra $50 a month, the representative of the mutual fund company chose an investment for her. It was fast and automatic.

Fund Supermarkets

One of the complaints of investors is the way their investments are scattered across a number of funds and brokerages. In response, many investment companies now offer discount brokerage and asset management. They also allow investors to invest in mutual funds from other fund families. These companies can be considered fund "supermarkets" because they allow you to purchase, consolidate, and manage your total portfolio in a sort of one-stop-shopping environment.

Top Three Fund Supermarkets

1. Fidelity Investments—Funds Network
2. Schwab Brokerage—One Source
3. T. Rowe Price—Mutual Fund Gateway

Discount Brokers

For many years, brokerage firms all charged the same commission for buying and selling stock. All of this changed in the early 1980s, when a law was passed allowing brokers to set their own prices. The floodgates opened, and the discount brokerage industry was born. Discount brokers were originally "bare-bones" brokers. They now offer many of the same services as their full-service competitors. The two largest discount brokers are ...

1. Schwab Discount Brokerage.
2. Fidelity Brokerage Services.

These two firms are really hybrids; they sell mutual funds as well as stocks and bonds, an advantage that they have over other firms. The other advantage is that you can visit their investor centers and speak to a financial representative in person. Schwab has more investor centers, but Fidelity has the largest selection and variety of mutual funds. Their services have expanded tremendously in the past several years to meet the demands of the individual investor.

There was a time when account representatives in these firms were simply order-takers. Today they do a much better job of guiding investors through the financial maze. They can help you determine what type of investment or service within their organization can best meet your needs. They can also provide you with research on stocks and bonds, and offer estate planning, asset management, and insurance.

When Kasey decided to invest in a specific stock, in addition to her mutual fund investment, she first opened a discount brokerage account. She knew what she wanted to purchase and wasn't really looking for anyone to make a recommendation. She used a discount broker who transacted business through the mail.

She requested and completed an account application, which she returned with a check. When the application was received, a representative from the firm called to confirm receipt and to ask her to place her order over the phone. All of these transactions were recorded, and a confirmation on the purchase was sent to Kasey. This is standard in the industry. By law, customers have three days to deliver funds to pay for the purchase.

Discount brokers often require payment up front if you are trading for the first time. At this stage, Kasey was more interested in an inexpensive transaction than personal service. Commissions on stocks have come down considerably in the past few years, and, depending upon how active a trader you are, you can often negotiate the price down further.

Full-Service Firms

Full-service firms get their name because that's what they offer investors: full service. It's considered a traditional model, but one that many investors still believe in. Full-service firms offer the investor a personal representative who oversees her portfolio. The broker calls her with investment recommendations, and for this service she pays a higher commission (the broker is paid a commission for each transaction that a client makes). An investor can call her broker at any time and be kept informed about the market or place an order. Over the years, a close relationship can develop.

Relationships are at the core of the full-service firm. Someone who knows your personal circumstances and history can, in theory, better attend to your needs. At a discount brokerage, any representative can take your order. The full-service model existed for years, but only high-net-worth investors had the privilege of using a personal broker.

An advantage that full-service firms offer clients is the firm's ability to participate in the underwriting of stock issues. As a result, the firm's clients are made privy to IPOs. Very few discount brokers underwrite new issues, although recently Fidelity and Schwab have established relationships that permit them access to these offerings.

The increased competition with discount brokers has caused these full-service, or full-cost, firms to change their compensation model. Many brokers are now compensated based on the amount of assets that a customer has with the firm. This is why many full-service brokers will consider working only with very high-asset clients.

Three of the largest full-service firms are ...

1. Merrill Lynch.
2. Morgan Stanley Dean Witter.
3. Salomon Smith Barney.

Coaching Tip

Large mutual funds aren't always better. They can be difficult to manage if they get too big. This is why Janus Funds closed several funds in 2000. They got too big to manage.

As Kasey's financial life evolved, her situation became more complex. She needed a higher level of assistance. Although she was comfortable researching stock herself, she welcomed the help of an expert who could make suggestions and recommendations on her behalf. As her portfolio grew, it required the assistance of someone who would stay on top of the market and inform her of any changes that might affect the stocks in her portfolio.

Kasey selected a full-service firm at this point in her investment path because it best suited her needs and goals.

Online Trading

Online trading has exploded as a result of the Internet. Initially, many of the discount brokerage firms allowed you to trade electronically by providing you with software that linked to their computer network. Discount brokers were the first to provide this service because their customers were accustomed to making investments on their own. It allowed firms to eliminate the amount of time their representatives spent on the phone taking orders.

The Internet was the catalyst that forced full-service firms to start providing online trading to their customers. Because this new Internet tool provided universal access to their customers, the full-service firms had to jump on board or be left behind.

The investor is now in the driver's seat because the competition is stiff. Both discount brokers and full-service firms offer online trading. Some firms are strictly online discount brokers. Here's a list of the top five in each category, according to www.gomez.com, the e-commerce authority Web site.

Full-Service Brokers Online

Firm	Score
1. Merrill Lynch	7.09
2. Morgan Stanley Dean Witter	6.41
3. Paine Webber	6.09
4. Salomon Smith Barney	5.35
5. Prudential Securities	5.31

(As of fall 2000)

Discount Brokers Online

Firm	Score
1. Charles Schwab	7.81
2. E*Trade	7.58
3. Fidelity Investments	7.22
4. DLJdirect	7.04
5. TD Waterhouse	6.93

(As of fall 2000)

To be included in the Internet Broker Scorecard, a firm must offer browser-based Internet trading.

Scorecards evaluate firms based on up to 150 or more objective criteria. These criteria are selected by Gomez experts to capture the quality of the Internet delivery of goods and services for a given sector. The highest score is 10 and the lowest is 0. (To see a complete and up-to-date ranking of online brokers, visit www.gomez.com.)

Smart Money magazine also comes out with an extensive annual ranking of brokers (visit www.smartmoney.com).

Financial Planning Firms

Kasey's financial life became even more complex after she started a business. She now had to provide her own retirement plan and deal with tax reporting and accounting. In addition, she had insurance needs, both personally and for her business. She was extremely pleased with her broker and the results that they had achieved. She asked him if he would refer her to someone who had expertise in small business. He agreed to recommend someone.

In the meantime, Kasey continued to network within her local chamber of commerce, which recommended a financial planner who specialized in helping businesses who were members. Kasey met with a certified financial planner, who was also a certified public accountant. He developed a plan for her, charging an hourly fee for his services. His expertise addressed her tax-reporting and -planning issues. He discussed establishing a Keogh retirement plan for her business and other types of strategies that she could use to address her insurance needs. The actual investments were still handled by Kasey's broker, which she preferred because she had established a wonderful rapport and relationship with him.

Coaching Tip

Your financial planner is your quarterback. She knows all about you and she will help you with your other advisers such as lawyers and accountants.

As a person's financial needs gain complexity, developing a team of advisers is the best approach. (See Chapter 17, "Selecting Your Best Advisers," for more on working with a team of advisers.) Financial planning firms offer a number of different services and frequently have specialists on staff to work on your team. This enables the financial planning firm to assist you in creating these plans:

- ❖ Financial plans
- ❖ Estate plans
- ❖ Business plans

Most financial planners are independent professionals who work outside of a firm. Here are the two of the largest national financial planning firms:

1. American Express Financial Advisers
2. Lincoln Financial Advisers

Money Therapy

Olivia Mellan

Many women are intimidated about finding good advisers and creating strong relationships that work for them. Because so many of us have been raised to be accommodating and pleasant and to avoid conflict, we tend to give away our power. Instead, remember that we are in the driver's seat in searching for help with our money.

Investing Through Your Bank

Banks are now becoming a one-stop shop for financial products and services. It's not uncommon to deposit funds in your bank account and be asked by a teller if you're interested in earning a higher return on your deposits.

Banks set up broker/dealer subsidiaries to sell investment products to their customers. One of the challenges facing banks is that people consider their bank deposits to be safe and insured. Securities, on the other hand, carry risk to your principal and are not covered by the FDIC insurance that bank deposits offer.

Originally, the Glass-Steagall Act made it illegal for banks to sell securities. Now legal, securities selling by banks is common. Banks offer investment services and sell discount brokerage, mutual funds, and insurance. Financial consultants or representatives on the premises can assist customers with investments. However, the account is treated like a brokerage account, and your investment relationship is kept separate from your banking relationship.

Banks offer convenience and liquidity if you need access to your investments. Most do not have in-house research and operate similarly to a discount broker. The representatives provide customers with choices and do not make recommendations on individual stocks or securities. Most bank products, however, do have sales charges associated with them and the representatives are paid on commission.

Three of the largest banks with investment services are ...

1. Bank of America.
2. Citibank.
3. First Union.

Kasey's financial journey was a process. Each time her needs changed, she was quick to search for the relationship that would meet those needs. She was truly in charge of her own financial success.

Where you invest will be determined by the relationships you forge and the needs you have at given points on your investment path.

The Bottom Line

Where you invest will be determined by what your needs are and will change as your financial life evolves. The most important decision is to invest somewhere.

Reader's Journal:

Knowledge Gained:

_____

_____

_____

_____

_____

_____

_____

_____

_____

_____

Steps I Will Take:

_____

_____

_____

_____

_____

_____

_____

_____

_____

_____

Stephanie is an accomplished journalist, single, attractive, and confident. She was raised to be a saver by parents who modeled it. In fact, when it comes to squeezing everything from a dollar, Stephanie does it.

In the past several years, Stephanie has amassed a significant amount of money in her savings accounts. She has invested in her employer's 401(k) plan and employee stock purchase program. Recently, Stephanie realized that while she was an excellent saver, she had not developed the skill set to be a good investor.

One reason she hesitated to invest (apart from her 401[k]) was a result of her job as a reporter. She reported on the stock market only when it experienced a dramatic high or low. This gave her the impression that the market was dangerous. Most of her $60,000 in savings was in the form of certificates of deposit, or CDs. On a recent visit to her bank, the teller noted her balance and suggested that she might want to sit down with an investment representative and consider alternatives.

Stephanie knew that she needed to do something, but she wasn't comfortable talking with a stranger about her savings. She was disturbed that the teller had access to her balance. But the teller's question did trigger Stephanie's determination to at least explore investing as a possibility. Subsequently, she asked a few friends what types of investments they were making and asked if they could refer her to an adviser. She was embarrassed to admit that she didn't know how to invest. She didn't realize how many men and women don't.

Stephanie liked the security and safety of her CDs. She could count on the interest being credited like clockwork. Her principal was always safe, and she didn't have to worry. However, her money hadn't been growing as rapidly as it had when she first bought her CDs. She was unhappy with the return but knew that if she invested in the stock market, she would have to give up her safety net.

Stephanie had accumulated a lump sum of money and was thankful, but she wondered if there was an investment that could pay her a higher return without her taking on more risk.

Chapter 12

Managing Your Unseen Forces

The Bottom Line

Money carries risk no matter where you put it. Choose your risk, and live with it.

Types of Risk

Becoming comfortable with risk and understanding the different types of risks are essential to becoming a financially confident woman. How do you overcome the fear of risk? With knowledge and experience.

There are four different types of risk:

1. Principal risk
2. Interest rate risk

3. Inflation risk

4. Market risk

In other words, whatever you decide to do with your money, there's risk associated with it. Even doing nothing carries a significant risk.

Principal Risk

Stephanie's refusal to invest was a result of her fear of losing her principal (the money she had in the bank). She, like so many others, was more concerned with preserving her savings than growing it, and with keeping it safe than keeping it working. There was no risk to her $60,000 in CDs because the bank provided FDIC insurance up to $100,000. The bank agreed to pay her interest for the term she agreed to, from six months on out to many years. Stephanie experienced a tremendous amount of comfort in this type of investment because safety was her biggest concern. But like it or not, Stephanie was exposing herself to serious risk—ironically, because she didn't want to risk her principal.

Interest Rate Risk

Stephanie was so aware of principal risk that she didn't consider interest rate risk. If she agreed to purchase a long-term CD, let's say, for two to three years, at a particular interest rate, she could run the risk of interest rates rising, in which case she would be stuck earning her lower rate. If she decided to redeem her CD before maturity, she would be assessed an early withdrawal penalty. Remember, every investment approach has its advantages and disadvantages. Stephanie's decision to invest in CDs carried the risk of falling victim to rising interest rates, exposing her to another kind of risk: inflation.

Inflation Risk

Inflation is what happens when the price of goods and services rises, reducing the buying power of a dollar. To counteract the rise in prices, your interest on savings must keep up with the rate of inflation. In the past decade, inflation has been kept to less than 3 percent a year. Yet even with low inflation, the price of certain goods has doubled in 10 years. For example, the average cost of a loaf of bread was 89 cents in 1990. Ten years later, it costs twice that.

Coaching Tip

Doing nothing with your money is the biggest risk of all.

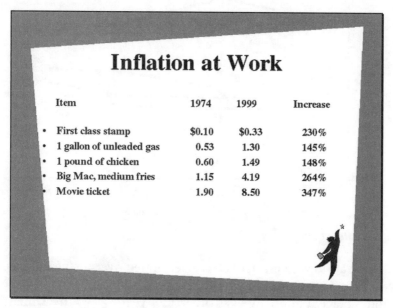

Inflation at Work

Item	1974	1999	Increase
• First class stamp	$0.10	$0.33	230%
• 1 gallon of unleaded gas	0.53	1.30	145%
• 1 pound of chicken	0.60	1.49	148%
• Big Mac, medium fries	1.15	4.19	264%
• Movie ticket	1.90	8.50	347%

Inflation chart.

While Stephanie's CDs were sitting safely in the bank earning 5 percent, both her investment and her interest were losing purchasing power. Simply put, her money would buy less in the future. So how does a person beat inflation? Well, it requires assuming another type of risk: market risk.

Coaching Tip

Your money has to make enough to pay for taxes and inflation and then some.

Market Risk

Is there any type of investment that has outpaced inflation over the years? Yes. The one type of investment that has consistently beaten inflation is stock. This is not the answer that people like Stephanie like to hear, however.

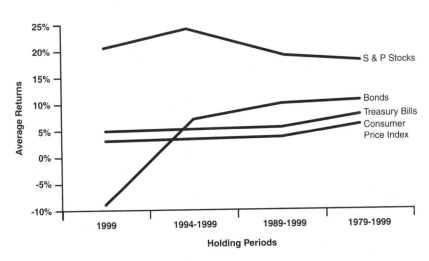

Historical rates of return.

If we look at how investments have performed over the years, we can have a much better idea of what to expect. Inflation has averaged around 3 percent annually over the last 74 years. Fixed investments such as CDs have averaged a mere 5 percent. Now let's look at the whole picture here. Stephanie earns 5 percent. We subtract inflation and end up with 2 percent. Then we take the taxes that she has to pay on these investments every year, even though she's rolling the money into new CDs at maturity, and her real rate of return is somewhere around 1 percent. Amazing, yes.

Is this a risk you should weigh when you make investment decisions? Absolutely. Your purchasing power is being eaten away slowly. To have a fighting chance of beating inflation, what do you have to do? Immerse yourself in market risk.

Stephanie was exposed to market risk through the investments she had made through her employer. The contributions in her employer's 401(k) plan were invested in stock mutual funds and company stock. She was familiar with the concept of investing in stock, but in her mind, the money she had invested for retirement was a long way off and didn't require much attention. She had experienced a significant increase in the value of those accounts and felt quite comfortable investing her money there.

Stephanie had succumbed to a common 401(k) malady: detachment. If I don't see it happening, it isn't important enough to worry about. She felt that her employer must know what he was doing, so she would trust him. Interestingly enough, she had been vulnerable to market risk all along through her 401(k) investments, but she didn't feel those vulnerabilities because it was money that she was detached from. In the period of time that Stephanie had been investing in her 401(k), the market had been up, down, and sideways, but she didn't let it affect her. She had invested right through the crash of 1987 and the turmoil of the early 1990s. Her investments in her employer's 401(k) had outpaced her CDs. Yet somehow, Stephanie hadn't made the connection.

Study the preceding chart. See how stocks have returned an average of almost 12 percent for the last 75 years? And the past 10 years have been even more remarkable: The average person's stock portfolio has returned more than 20 percent. The average fixed investment, such as a savings account or a CD, has returned less than 4 percent in the same period. Is past investment activity a guarantee of the future? No, but it probably isn't something that anyone should ignore.

It's probably a good idea to invest in both fixed investments and stocks. My job was to alert Stephanie to the fact that her CDs and 401(k) were all pieces of the financial pie and should be approached based on the overall goals that she was trying to achieve. For Stephanie, the goal was financial independence. She had to realize that she was losing money by having only fixed investments. It was the only approach that would make sense to her and create the urgency that she needed to move forward.

When Stephanie called me and asked about the funds that I had suggested at our last meeting, I decided to act. I asked, "Why didn't you invest after our last meeting?" She listed her excuses, chiefly that the adviser she had spoken with would take a commission.

I said, "Your fears are losing you money. In the six months since we talked, those mutual funds that I suggested are up more than 20 percent." She gasped, "That's why I called. I've been watching the market in the news and feeling really silly about not doing anything." She was finally ready but still lacked confidence.

Money Therapy

Olivia Mellan

If you're someone who lacks confidence when it comes to money and investing, realize that you are far from alone. Most women's lack of confidence around money comes from old messages that were handed down from generation to generation about men being better than we are when it comes to investing.

To gain the confidence, she needed to grasp that she was already an experienced investor through her 401(k) plan. She needed to engage herself in the plan, to take an active role in its growth. First, she looked at her 401(k) investments to get a sense of how they had performed since her enrollment in the plan. How much money had she made? What type of stocks were her mutual funds invested in? Which companies was she familiar with? I gave her a week to find this information and give me a call back. Do you think she called?

Yes, she did, three days later. She was motivated now because she wanted her money to grow. She had called her plan administrator to assess how her plan had performed over time. She also asked to be sent a "Morningstar Mutual Fund Report" on each of the funds that she owned. A whole new world was opening to her. Stephanie realized that she was already a successful investor. She was familiar with many of the companies that were top holdings in her mutual funds. When she compared her savings in CDs to the performance of her 401(k) portfolios, it was a wake-up call. Her money in her plan had quadrupled, and although she had saved a good deal, there was no comparison. Stephanie was fired up.

Stephanie inquired whether she could invest in some of those same mutual funds outside of her portfolio. We discussed some of those funds and the fact that she had a significant amount with one investment company, that it might be a good idea to spread the wealth and invest in another fund. We narrowed her choices to two funds and printed out applications from the Internet over the phone. I reviewed with her how to fill out the applications and had her set up automatic monthly deposits. Her transition from fear to confidence was remarkable.

Since then, Stephanie has weathered the market. She understands the investment process. She has learned to manage her unseen forces.

Coaching Tip

Education is the key to investing. We fear what we don't understand. Once we understand, we know how to avoid the pitfalls.

Other Types of Risk

In addition to the four types of risk described, you should be familiar with two other types: life transition risk and unresolved money issues risk.

Life Transition Risk

There is another risk none of us can control: life transitions. We never know when our lives will change and we will be vulnerable to financial disaster.

Preparing for the worst, yet believing that the best will happen, is a mature view. It will prompt you to make choices that will give you the best financial protection possible.

Opportunity knocks, partners leave, illness strikes, death happens, jobs end. The average age of widowhood today is 56. I see it happening before my eyes at church, as more and more women outlive their husbands. Many of them were middle-class and unprepared for disaster even though their husbands were loving providers. The right questions weren't asked, or the papers weren't signed.

Money Therapy

Olivia Mellan

Remember that most of us will be alone at some time in our lives, and that half of marriages end in divorce in our culture. Since we can't predict life's changes, we have to be prepared for them to proceed in life with a sense of true security and stability—and true peace of mind.

Unresolved Money Issues Risk

Here is another risk that is often overlooked in conversations about investing: unresolved money issues. There is a lot to be said about this. Most experts agree that we impose financial limitations upon ourselves by following old ways of thinking that we adopted along the way.

One common thinking error, for example, is that money is evil; wanting more of it means that you are greedy. This is not true. Money isn't evil. It is neither evil nor good—it just is. Evil and good can both be expressed using money, but money is just money. Wanting more money doesn't mean that you're greedy; it means that you understand how useful it is for living the life you plan. If you're greedy, you'll be greedy with or without money.

Another common thinking error is that people with money are arrogant and selfish. Do you know any arrogant and selfish people who don't have much money? Of course you do. So do I. If you're concerned that people will like you less if you have enough money, ask yourself if those people will take care of you financially when you need it. Like yourself, and let others take care of themselves.

Manage your unseen forces. Step beyond what you don't know. Identify your fears and misperceptions, and pursue confidence as an investor.

The Bottom Line

To be a confident investor, you have to face whatever fear is holding you back.

Reader's Journal:

Knowledge Gained:

_____

_____

_____

_____

_____

_____

_____

_____

_____

_____

Steps I Will Take:

_____

_____

_____

_____

_____

_____

_____

_____

_____

_____

Cynthia can remember her mother forcing her to open an IRA for $500 the first summer she worked as a lifeguard in high school. She made a cool $1,000 and watched half of it go into what, to a teenager, seemed like a black hole.

The following Christmas, her mother handed her an envelope. Inside was an IRA mutual fund statement with Cynthia's name on it in the amount of $1,100. Cynthia's mother had matched the $500 that Cynthia had originally invested, and the extra $100 was the appreciation of the fund since it was acquired.

Cynthia was impressed that she had more than doubled her money. Her mother agreed to continue matching Cynthia's annual IRA investment each year. It set the stage for a lifetime of investing.

Fifteen years have passed since that first Christmas. Cynthia's IRA now totals more than $80,000. As a result of her IRA experience, she did not hesitate to invest in the retirement plans that were offered through her employer. She felt very comfortable reviewing the options and choosing more aggressive funds. Cynthia is in her early 30s now. Her investment portfolio is valued at more than $200,000. She attributes her success to her mother, who retired from the teaching profession at the age of 50 and is pursuing her first love of writing.

Chapter 13

Investing for Retirement

The Bottom Line

It's never too late, or too early, to plan for the life you will live after
you retire.

There are two aspects to retirement planning: before you retire
and after you retire, or pre- and post-retirement planning. If you
are a potential retiree, there are several lifestyle decisions that
you will want to make as part of your planning process. If you
are an actual retiree, you need to consider what effect the choices
you have made for your retired life will have on your portfolio.
And while no decision should be entered into hastily, you'll need
to keep an open mind about a number of issues that you may
have thought were set in stone.

Preretirement Planning

If you are still working, it's time to think about what you want your life to be like when you're retired. Really think about it. Look at retired people around you, and decide whether you'd like to live like any of them. Choose your heroes. If you don't find any, create your own. Define the life you want.

Avoid saying, "I want to live comfortably." It's too vague and won't motivate you. Instead say, "I want to be in my own home, travel four times a year within the country and one time abroad, have an ample book and garden budget, and be able to afford the food, vitamins, and prescriptions necessary for excellent health. I want a car in good repair that can easily transport me wherever I want to go, and I want to be able to slip small bills to the family when the mood strikes me."

In financial terms, this would be called a retirement planning goal. What is yours? Rewrite the last paragraph to describe the life you want when you retire.

Well-Defined Retirement

A well-defined retirement planning goal is specific and includes answers to these questions:

1. How long do you have left before you want to retire?
2. How long do you expect to be retired?
3. How much do you currently earn each year?
4. How much of your current annual earnings will you need when you retire?
5. How much have you already accumulated toward your retirement?
6. How much do you regularly add to those investments?
7. Do your investments match the return you need, or are you invested too conservatively?

An Example

Let's say that you're 45 and want to retire at 65. That's 20 years. According to statistics, you should live to about age 85. But let's say that people in your family tend to live longer. We'll make your life expectancy 90. That means we're trying to plan for 25 years of retirement, from age 65 to 90.

Let's say that you currently make $30,000 per year. When you retire, your clothing and commuting expenses will decrease. But remember, your insurance, healthcare, and travel expenses will probably increase. The general estimate is that you'll need around 80 percent of your pre-retirement income to maintain your standard of living after you stop working. Let's make a more conservative assumption and say that you'll need 90 percent. That works out to $27,000.

You already have $50,000 in your company's 401(k) and another $25,000 in your traditional IRA. In addition, you've saved $10,000 in a money market account at the bank.

You regularly put 10 percent of your pay into the 401(k), but you've made your IRA contribution only sporadically.

Your 401(k) is currently invested 50 percent in the stable value fund and 50 percent in the company's stock because that's how it pays the match. Your IRA is invested in a U.S. government bond fund, and your money market at the bank pays about 2 percent.

This gives us what we need—a goal that defines your needs in terms of the following:

Time (how long you have to achieve it)

Duration (how long you need the income)

Amount (how much you need)

Now that the goal is set, let's look at the rest of the information in this example.

Time

First, the clock, or the calendar, is still your friend. With 20 more years to work, you will want to consider being more aggressive with your investments.

Life Expectancy

Second, you're planning to live a long time in retirement. This means that you're aiming to accumulate an even larger nest egg to pay for that long retirement. It also means that post-retirement inflation is a very real issue for you, so remember to include stocks in your portfolio, even after you have completely stopped working.

Retirement Budget

Third, work out a budget for yourself—both a current budget and a projected retirement budget. Put everything in it: haircuts, manicures, restaurant meals, movies, and all those trips to Starbucks. All these little expenses add up quickly. Figure out exactly where your money is going now, and try to determine where it will probably go when you stop working. This will help you determine how much income you'll need when you retire. If you have some expensive goals, such as travel, be sure to include that in your budget. This may mean that you need more than 100 percent of your pre-retirement income for a few years after you retire. But don't expect to keep up that pace of spending for very long. It's a quick way to wind up back at work.

Estimate Inflation

Fourth, project out your estimated income need for inflation. Here, your goal is to have the equivalent of $27,000 a year in income when you retire. But that's going to be 25 years from now. At 4 percent inflation, that $27,000 today is the same as $72,000 when you retire. Before you groan and say that's a crazy number, remember how crazy it would have sounded to say we'd be paying 33¢ for postage stamps back in the early 1970s, when we were paying just 8¢.

Size of Your Nest Egg

The next step is to figure out what size nest egg you need to pay that income for as long as you want it. In this case, you're looking for a $73,000 annual income to be paid for the 25 years that you expect to be retired. Using a very conservative 4 percent rate of return, you'll need about $1,200,000. Oh boy! That's more money than you ever planned on putting together.

How to Get There

But before you say that this is impossible, let's look at exactly how you *can* get there. You've already accumulated $75,000 in 401(k) and IRA accounts, and it has 20 more years to grow before you need it. Currently, you're contributing to the 401(k) plan at work, and that's great. But be aware of your vesting schedule. Employees these days tend to have seven or eight jobs throughout their working lives. If you quit your job before you're fully vested, you could leave behind a big chunk of money. And that could have a dramatic effect on your retirement.

Then there's the issue of how to invest the money in your 401(k) and IRA accounts. Unfortunately, stable value and money market accounts don't do a very good job of keeping pace with inflation, let alone growing fast enough to help you get ahead. In general, women have a habit of investing far too conservatively. You've reviewed the historical performance of asset classes and now realize that if your time frame is seven or more years, stocks have historically performed better.

In our example, you have half the money in the stable value fund. Sounds like that decision needs to be rethought, taking inflation into account. But taking on the stock market doesn't mean putting all your money into company stock, either. When the stock is going up, nobody seems to think it's a bad idea. But when the stock isn't doing so well, you can better appreciate the need for diversification. The problem is, you never know how the stock is going to behave or when. Of course, if your employer pays its match in company stock and gives you no alternative, then you will have to work around that.

Coaching Tip

If you have your 401(k) money invested in your company stock, you are at risk. Think about it. You have your current living invested in that company because they give you your paycheck. You also have your future living invested in that company. Sounds too risky to me. If you can diversify your 401(k), do it. And think very hard before you participate in the employee stock purchase plan.

Help for the Money Market Account

The $10,000 that you have in a money market account at the bank needs some help. If this is your rainy day money, you need a better money market fund. If this money is intended to supplement your retirement savings efforts, you need to look at something with better growth potential.

In this example, you regularly put 10 percent of your pay into the 401(k). Familiarize yourself with the elements of your 401(k) plan. Each one has slightly different rules. But some of the rules are the same from plan to plan. For one, you can contribute a maximum of 15 percent of your pay to the plan. If you're below that, especially if you have ground to make up, raise your 401(k) contribution amount. By making your contributions sooner in your life rather than later, your money has longer to compound. This way you make the clock your friend, not your enemy. In Chapter 3, "The Confident Investor," we provide a chart on how time can impact compound growth.

If you take nothing else from this chapter, take this: No matter what you do with your employer's retirement plan, you can always contribute to some type of IRA—and you should. If you've only made your IRA contribution sporadically, as in the example, make it a priority to contribute the full $2,000 a year regularly. Make the payments monthly, quarterly, or annually—but make them.

The Four Retirement Buckets

Another way to look at how you can save and invest for retirement is to look at the types of dollars you can use. Always try to go from the most efficient to the least efficient type. Four types of money can be used for this purpose:

1. Pretax matched money
2. Pretax unmatched money
3. After-tax tax-deferred money
4. Taxable money

Think of these money types as buckets that should be filled in sequence. Each bucket has a limit on how much you can put into it, so put everything that you can into bucket #1 before you put anything into bucket #2, and so on.

First Bucket

Bucket #1 is pretax, matched money. Here, you get three benefits: pretax contributions, matching money from your employer, and tax deferral on all your investment earnings. First, your contribution is made before federal and state income taxes, so you have to earn only $1 to contribute $1. (See the taxable section [bucket #4] to compare.) Second, because you put your own money in, your employer will give you free money to go with your own contribution. I don't know about you, but if I'm offered free money, I take it! Whether you get to keep this employer contribution when you quit this job will depend on whether you are "vested." Third, you get to realize all the investment gains you want, and you pay no tax at that time. All the taxes are put off until you withdraw from these accounts.

A word about vesting: You always get to keep your own contributions to the plan, plus what that money has grown to. Once you're vested, you get to keep the company's contributions, too. Each 401(k) plan has different rules about when an employee becomes vested. The schedule will be either "cliff" or "graded." With a cliff vesting schedule, there's one length of time, and once you've been employed with the company for that long, you're vested. For instance, with a three-year cliff vesting schedule, once you have three years of time in service with your employer, you are fully vested. If you quit with two years and 364 days, you are not vested at all. With a graded vesting schedule, you become progressively more vested each year. For example, with a four-year vesting schedule, you become 25 percent vested each year. After four years, you are fully vested.

So, before you decide to take a new job, be aware of what you may give up in unvested benefits. And if you're close to meeting the vesting requirement, consider sticking it out until you do. It could make a big difference.

There are two kinds of accounts in which you would take advantage of pretax matched money. If you're a private-sector employee, it's the part of your 401(k) that your company matches you on, usually the first few percent of salary. If you are a FERS government employee, then it refers to your Thrift Savings Plan (TSP).

One question that often comes up is whether contributing to these kinds of plans will have any effect on your Social Security or Medicare benefits. The answer is an unequivocal "no" because you still pay both Social Security and Medicare taxes on the money that you contribute to the plan. This way there is no reduction in these benefits.

Second Bucket

Bucket #2 is pretax, unmatched money. This means that you still get the tax deduction, but no one gives you any free money to go along with it. Plus, you get tax-deferred growth. The pretax aspect is a very big benefit, so be sure to take full advantage of it. This is usually the full complement of your 401(k) contribution. So, if your employer matches you on only the first 5 percent of your contribution, this would be the additional 10 percent that you can put in.

Depending on your adjusted gross income (AGI), it may be your traditional IRA contribution as well. If you make less than $40,000 as a single taxpayer, or less than $60,000 as a married taxpayer (regardless of whether you file separately or jointly), then you can deduct a portion of your traditional IRA contribution. If you make more, you can still make a traditional IRA contribution—you just won't be able to deduct it.

Third Bucket

Bucket #3 is after-tax, tax-deferred money. Here, you don't get a tax deduction, but you do get to have your money grow, and you don't pay taxes on those earnings as you go along. You pay income tax on these funds only when you withdraw from the account.

The kinds of accounts that you would find in bucket #3 include Roth IRAs, fixed annuities, variable annuities, and traditional IRAs for people over the AGI limits for deductibility.

Let's stop to talk about Roth IRAs. A Roth IRA works much like a traditional IRA, with a couple of notable exceptions. First, to be eligible for a Roth, your AGI must be under $95,000 as a single taxpayer, or below $110,000 as a married taxpayer filing jointly. Married taxpayers who file separately are not currently eligible to have a Roth IRA.

Second, there is no possibility of deducting your $2,000 annual contribution. Roth contributions are by definition after-tax money.

Third, when you are over age 59$^{1}/_2$, you can withdraw from your Roth with no income taxes. And unlike traditional IRAs, a Roth IRA has no required minimum distribution when you reach age 70$^{1}/_2$. This is a huge benefit. If you are eligible both for a Roth IRA and for a deductible traditional IRA, talk with your financial adviser about which would be best for you. You can put only a total of $2,000 into an IRA each year, regardless of the type, so it's important to make the most of that limited contribution.

Fourth Bucket

Bucket #4 is taxable investments. This category is usually the one that most people think of first when they think of investing. And it does represent some important assets that you will gather over the course of your life, including your home, your "rainy day" money market account, your company's employee stock purchase plan shares, and your qualified or incentive stock options. These are important pools of money to collect. But you have to be aware of the effect that federal and state taxes will have on how you manage these assets. To begin with, if you are in the 31 percent federal income tax bracket, you will have to earn $1.44 to have $1 to invest after you've paid your federal taxes. Obviously, state taxes will add to this burden.

Also, consider carefully whether the assets that you gather here are for investment purposes or for your personal use. The most obvious point for discussion here is your home. If you intend to live in it after retirement, then it is a personal use asset. If you intend to sell it and use the proceeds to make income-producing investments, then it is more of an investment. Keep this distinction in mind as you calculate what assets you have that will be available to fund your retirement income needs.

Post-Retirement Strategies

First, what does retirement mean to you? It may include travel, volunteering, or part-time employment. There are at least seven areas that need to be examined closely.

Budget and Net Worth

You have to make ends meet, so take some time and draw up a budget. Know how much you will be receiving in income and how much it takes for you to live each month. Find out what you expect your Social Security benefits to be and when you expect to begin taking them. Will you be drawing a pension? How much will it be, and when will it start? Will you be working part-time?

On the expense side, don't forget to include those little expenses such as haircuts and pocket money that you might now take for granted. And remember those expenses that are likely to become a larger part of your budget as you get older, including prescription costs, health insurance premiums, and supplemental insurance costs. And remember to budget for your vacation! You will still need one, even after you retire.

Net worth is simply an accounting of what you own and what you owe. Officially, the equation is this:

Assets – liabilities = net worth

Sit down and figure out what your net worth is. While you're looking at the list, think about how you want to use those assets during retirement. Do you expect your assets to provide your income completely so that you can "live off the interest"? Or, do you anticipate that in generating your retirement income, you will deplete your assets—either partially or completely?

Coaching Tip

It's a good idea to wait until retirement to pay off your house. You can decide within a year or so if you don't want to have a house payment. The trade off is having your money in your house or in an investment account. If your house is truly an appreciating asset, it makes sense. If not, think about it. But if paying it off makes you feel more secure, pay attention to your feelings.

Housing

The big question here is twofold:

- ❖ Do you want to live in the same city where you currently live?
- ❖ Do you want to live in a large house, or will a smaller home do?

Just because you've retired doesn't mean that you have to move. So, before you rush to buy a home in a new city, you may want to try out the city for more than just a week or two, particularly at that city's least appealing time.

I knew a woman named Jan who lived in Washington, D.C., for 40 plus years. When her husband retired, they moved to Scottsdale, Arizona. They chose Scottsdale because that was where they thought they were "supposed" to go. They had been there on business trips, but never for an extended period of time, and certainly not in July or August. Jan discovered that she found it unbearably hot during the summer. And she hated the place because she didn't know anyone there. When her husband died, she immediately moved back to Washington.

That's an expensive and painful lesson to learn—that they probably shouldn't have moved to Arizona in the first place. So, consider very carefully your decision to move to a new city when you retire. It's a long-term move.

Lyn's Retirement

The other question has to do with the size, style, and layout of your home. Your home has to fit both your physical and your emotional needs. Let's look at another woman, named Lyn. She and her husband lived in a lovely three-story federal home for 40 years. But at the age of 71, Lyn was tired of keeping up such a large house for only two people. And she knew that as she grew older, the stairs might become a real problem—not just for her, but also for her husband, for whom she would be the primary caregiver if he became ill. They wrestled with the issue of whether to leave the home in which they had raised their children. They knew that they would miss opening Christmas gifts in the old living room. But they also knew that they would never miss the ever-growing property tax bill.

Ultimately, they decided that the reduced housework, the easier mobility of a single-story condominium, and the opportunity to take cash out of a long paid-off mortgage would better suit their needs. So, they sold their four-bedroom house, bought a one-bedroom condominium, and invested the cash. And because they considered all their alternatives first and didn't make a hasty decision, they are very pleased with their retirement home.

Your Home

If you're considering selling your current home, remember, you can now sell your primary residence once every two years and recognize $500,000 in gains for a married couple or $250,000 for a single or widowed person, without paying any capital gains tax. If your retirement income looks like it may come up short, this may be a way for you to get your hands on some cash.

If you want to stay in your current home, you may need to consider refinancing your mortgage. This would give you cash for income-generating purposes, and it also would give you a home mortgage interest tax deduction.

Reverse Mortgage

You can also consider using a reverse mortgage to provide income if you remain in your current home. To take out a reverse mortgage, your home must be fully paid for. Then the bank makes monthly payments to you, for a period of years, or for as long as you live, depending on your contract. The amount of the payment depends on current interest rates and how long payments will be made to you. With a regular mortgage, you paid the bank each month. In this case, the bank pays you, and you can use the income for any purpose that you choose. But be aware that taking out a reverse mortgage means that you are giving up all or part of your ownership in the house. Depending on the terms of your reverse mortgage, the bank may own your home when you die, and your heirs may not be able to inherit it.

Social Security

The Social Security Administration (SSA) automatically sends out estimates of benefits to workers in years when their age ends in a "0" or "5." This Statement of Benefits outlines what the SSA expects to pay you and when (at age 62, 65/67, or 70). Double-check the SSA's records before you retire, and be sure that it has correct information on your earnings history. Take this information to your adviser, and determine what your anticipated benefits are, what your survivor benefits will be, and when you should start collecting. You can visit the Social Security Web site at www.ssa.gov for more information.

If you are divorced or widowed, and if both you and your former husband were eligible for Social Security benefits, you must make these decisions carefully because you can take only one benefit. You cannot take the lower benefit early and then switch to the higher benefit at a later date.

Taxes

Taxes are always an important issue. Goodness knows, they seem to take up an overwhelming proportion of everything we earn. When you change to the ranks of the retired, taxes seem to become even more important because you're on a more limited income. Remember, there are two kinds of taxes here: ordinary income taxes and capital gains taxes. Capital gains taxes are lower than ordinary income taxes.

You should look closely at the income that you will be receiving during retirement, and understand how those amounts will be taxed. This is a conversation best held with both your tax adviser/accountant and your investment adviser. These two professionals need to work together to maximize your income and minimize your tax liabilities. Each will probably be aware of a particular aspect of your situation that the other isn't, so getting them working together is critical to making the most of your money.

Taxed as Ordinary Income	Taxed as Capital Gains
Dividends	
Interest	
401(k)/IRA distributions	
Social Security benefits	
Employment income	
	Realized gains from capital appreciation

Insurance Coverage

The first question is what kind of insurance you need, and for what purpose. Do you need life insurance, health insurance, disability insurance, or long-term-care insurance? Why do you need it? Here are some typical reasons for owning various types of insurance.

Type of Insurance	Typical Reason for Buying It
Life insurance	Provide estate liquidity
	Pay for child/grandchild's college education
	Provide for a disabled child/relative
Health insurance	Not yet eligible for Medicare
	Want to cover expenses that Medicare doesn't
Disability insurance	Need to make up for lost employment income
Long-term-care insurance	Want to avoid depleting assets
	Need to mitigate family history of long illness
	Need to cover expenses that Medicare doesn't pay for
	Want to keep from relying on your children for home care or nursing home expenses

If you can get coverage through the employer from whom you retired, that will likely be your best alternative. The premiums may go up because of your status as a retiree. Depending on your employer, you may be able to get better access to company insurance coverage if you reduce your employment status to part-time instead of retiring. But remaining employed will likely affect other benefits, such as your ability to roll over your 401(k) balance to an IRA account.

You may also be able to get various kinds of insurance coverage through groups such as the American Association of Retired Persons (AARP), your labor union, or various professional societies. Ask the organizations that you are a member of what kinds of programs they offer. As always, read the information that they provide very closely to be sure that the coverage provides the benefits that you need and want.

You also need to consider whether you have "insurability" issues. Insurance companies generally will not write policies on those who are already ill or who have certain types of family histories. If you're unable to get insurance on your own, check with your children to see what benefits their employer plans may offer to you as an employee's parent. For example, some companies offer long-term-care insurance to their employees. And as an additional benefit, they offer coverage to the employee's parents, in-laws, and children. If you can access this kind of benefit, you may want to take advantage of it.

Heirs

I know it sounds like common sense, but be sure to do your estate planning. If you don't, you may leave your estate with a hefty but unexpected tax bill. And retirement account assets can be subject to both income and estate taxes if not properly handled. Estate taxes start at 35 percent and quickly escalate to 55 percent, with a nasty bump up to 60 percent for estates between $10 million and $21 million. So, if you're in the 39.6 percent federal tax bracket and the 8 percent state tax bracket, and if your estate is in the 55 percent bracket, your IRA could be subject to 103 percent tax upon your death. You wouldn't want your estate to owe more than the account is worth, so be sure that your plan takes into account your IRA balances, especially if they are a particularly large proportion of your estate.

Consider carefully who you want your heirs to be: your husband, your children, your parents or in-laws, your siblings, your nieces and nephews, charities, a local hospital, your alma mater, or maybe a family trust. Talk to your investment adviser, accountant, and attorney about the best way to get certain assets to those heirs—some assets receive special treatment when left to certain people. Plus, you will need to take taxes into consideration and make the most tax-efficient use of your assets. Many people set up a Charitable Remainder Trust that allows them to give appreciated assets to their church or other charitable organization and receive certain tax benefits. If you have financial needs that are complex you can learn more in *Everywoman's Money: Financial Freedom*. It covers these types of issues in more detail.

Asset Allocation

As you move into being fully retired, you will probably want to move more of your assets to bonds so that you can reliably generate the income stream that you need. But just because you've retired doesn't mean that inflation has gone away. To keep up with inflation, you need to maintain some stock or stock mutual funds in your portfolio. For example, let's say that you have $300,000 when you retire, and divide it into $250,000 in bonds and $50,000 in stocks. Several years later, the bonds are still worth $250,000 and are still pumping out the income. Meanwhile, the stocks have grown to $75,000. That means that you can harvest $25,000 in growth from those stocks and reallocate that money to bonds. Voilà! Instant retirement raise! That's how stocks help you keep up with inflation after you've retired.

Now, obviously, you won't want to be super-aggressive with those stock choices. But some good-quality growth, growth and income, or equity income alternatives would certainly be worth considering. The rule of diversification still applies to post-retirement stocks: some of each size (large-cap, mid-cap, small-cap), some different geography (Europe, Asia, Latin America), and some different styles (growth, GARP, value).

The Bottom Line

Your retirement dreams can be a reality, but you have to make them a priority. You deserve a wonderful retirement.

Reader's Journal:

Knowledge Gained:

_____

_____

_____

_____

_____

_____

_____

_____

_____

Steps I Will Take:

_____

_____

_____

_____

_____

_____

_____

_____

_____

Michael and Ava were new parents. They wanted to prepare for their child's future so that he wouldn't experience the financial difficulties that they faced in college.

They had a savings account at the bank and had invested in some mutual funds. Recently, their state introduced a prepaid college savings program. It required them to invest several thousand dollars but would guarantee their child's future tuition at a state college. It sounded like an excellent idea; however, they didn't have the six grand required for a newborn to enroll in the program.

On the other hand, their son was only six months old, and the longer they waited, the more expensive the program would become. Michael and Ava explored alternatives, including mutual funds. Many of them looked promising.

The unknown factor was how much college would cost 18 years from the time their son was an infant. They calculated an estimate and decided that the state's college plan was their best choice. They took out a five-year loan with monthly payments to pay for it.

Now, 13 years later, Kevin is starting high school. Michael and Ava are relieved that his college education is funded. Since enrolling in the college plan, the family has moved to another state. Michael was relieved to find out that the program will cover the national average of tuition cost at any public college.

This program worked so well for Michael and Ava that they repeated it for their newborn daughter.

Chapter 14

Investing for College

The Bottom Line

Paying for an education requires an intentional and consistent effort.

Ask any parent what the number-one goal for a child's education is, and most will tell you that they want their children to get a college degree. Currently, most jobs require a four-year degree. Jobs today are much more specialized than at any time in history. We live in an information age where what you know is what you are. Knowledge affects every aspect of our lives. For instance, the knowledge and use of computer software programs is not a specialized skill; it's a necessity. The trend in our third millennium is toward lifetime learning. It's no longer enough just to achieve a certain level of education; you must constantly upgrade your knowledge and skills.

I'm always amazed when I hear the statistic that employees who have completed a college degree program earn more than $1 million more over their working years than employees who have completed only high school. In other words, having a college degree is a big asset in the job market. In fact, a college degree is needed not only to compete for entry-level jobs, but also to advance in your career.

Even though most people know these facts, many still believe that a college education is just a dream. The cost of a college education has risen faster each year than the rate of inflation. As a matter of fact, in the middle 1990s the cost of college tuition rose an average of 8 percent annually. Thankfully, this trend has been controlled in the past few years, but college tuition still rises faster than the rate of inflation, which has been about 3 percent per year.

So, how can you afford college for you, your kids, or your grandkids? If your kids or grandkids are toddlers, you can put a small monthly amount in an investment and reap big rewards by college age. But what about upgrading your skills, getting an advanced degree such as an MBA, or helping your older kids get a college degree?

The good news is that there are many ways to pay for college, and they don't all involve an empty wallet or sacrificing other financial goals. With knowledge, planning, and saving, your dreams of a college education for yourself or a loved one are realistic.

Ways to Pay for College

There are three ways to pay the cost of a college education. These methods can be accomplished individually or in combination with one another.

Before College

The first method of funding a college education is saving and investing before entering college. The most common method is investing in one or more mutual funds. As you learned in Chapter 10, "How to Invest in Mutual Funds," mutual funds are shares of stock from many different companies that are all owned by a fund. By buying a share of a certain mutual fund, you own a very small number of shares of different companies.

Mutual funds are great for three reasons. A professional manager chooses and monitors the performance of these many companies, the risk is less because there are many different stocks in the fund, and most mutual fund companies have "wealth builder" accounts. These are accounts to which you contribute a minimum amount of money each month and, over time, buy more shares at different prices. Many people open an investment account when their child or grandchild is a newborn and then have a certain amount deducted from their bank account (usually the minimum is $25). By contributing regularly, you buy some shares when the fund price is low and some when the price is high, but it evens out over time. Also, by having the dividends re-invested, the number of shares in your account keeps increasing.

This is how you build wealth—and this will help you send your kids to college. Keep in mind that a savings account or CD at a bank usually pays only 2 percent to 5 percent, while a mutual fund may earn 10 percent or more per year.

During College

Some lucky students earn scholarships that help pay their tuition, board, and other expenses. Scholarships and grants are "free money" given for academic or athletic talent, or other reasons. Many students must take loans to help pay for their education. In fact, the average college student graduates college with $13,000 in debt. We'll discuss the different types of student loans in a moment. Just keep in mind that student loans are the last rung of the college funding ladder and should be used only when all other means of funding have been exhausted.

Some students actually "pay as they go" and have jobs while taking courses. They find jobs with area businesses in the local community. Usually students are paid a minimum wage that helps them meet the cost of food, clothing, and other living expenses. Students may also work at summer jobs and save for expenses that they will have during the next semester.

Work-study programs are available at most colleges. Each student works at a campus job administered by his or her school. Students in these programs work 10 to 20 hours per week. In 1999, the average yearly earnings per student in a work-study program were $1,120.

Coaching Tip

Be careful about taking equity out of your house. If you are forced into this decision, it may be that your home equity is your only asset. Don't spend it without really thinking about it. If you are a single mom with no other assets, I suggest you make the hard choice to let your child pay for her education herself.

After College

Repayment for most student loans begins after the student has graduated. Some loans require that the interest be paid immediately, but principal payments can begin later. Monthly loan repayments are calculated at a set interest rate over a certain time period, usually 10 years. Later we will talk in depth about the different types of loans and how a student or family can qualify.

Savings in Your Child's Name

When you establish an account in your child's name, the account belongs to your child. Children who are still considered minors must have someone over the age of 18 as the co-owner of the account. Therefore, you may open a savings account in your child's name, but you would actually be responsible for the account.

Let's take a look at some of the most popular ways to save for a child's college.

Savings bonds

A popular gift to children is a Series EE U.S. savings bond. A savings bond is purchased for half of the face value of the bond; a $50 bond costs $25. Bonds come in eight denominations from $50 up to 10,000 and can be bought at your local bank. Series EE savings bonds take 12 years to mature. When a bond matures, you may take it to the bank and receive the full face amount in cash. Savings bonds are a very safe method of saving, but the return is usually much lower than that of mutual funds or other investments.

Accounts in your child's name

Specific accounts can be established in a child's name, and the funds must be used only for the child. A parent or another adult must be named as trustee. These accounts are called either Uniform Gift to

Minors (UGMA) or Uniform Transfer to Minors (UTMA), depending upon the state where the child resides. UGMA/UTMA accounts have some definite advantages, the main one being that for children under age 14, the first $650 of yearly income from dividends or interest earned in the account is tax-free. Money can be deposited in the account at any time, and then stocks, bonds, mutual funds, insurance, and other investments may be purchased.

There is one disadvantage to this type of account: When the child reaches the "age of majority"—age 18 to 21, depending on the state— the child then owns the account and may spend the assets as he or she wants. This means that the child can use the money in the account to buy a car instead of paying for college tuition.

Coaching Tip

Whenever the IRS gives you a tax break, you lose control of your money. Make sure you know the regulations before you put any money into a tax-advantaged investment.

Education IRA

An education IRA is an investment account that is established specifically for college savings. Five hundred dollars per year can be deposited into this account for children under the age of 18. Contributions are not tax-deductible, so there is no immediate savings on income taxes. The good news is that the money and assets in this type of account grow tax-free. Even better, there are no taxes due when the money is withdrawn to pay for college. Money in an education IRA can be used to cover tuition, books, and room and board. Be aware that the tax-free aspect of the earnings and withdrawals are phased out at higher levels of income.

Other Sources

There are many other ways to save for college besides savings bonds, UGMAs, and UTMAs. Most people have a savings account in their own name.

Savings accounts

Accounts in the parent's or grandparent's name may be bank savings or investment accounts used to keep money for emergencies or for specific future events such as travel, college, or retirement. Investment accounts that are established with brokerage houses, mutual funds, and other companies can also be used for these purposes. Investment accounts may include life insurance with cash value, mutual funds, stocks, and bonds.

An advantage of having an account in your own name is that you will have complete control of the account and be able to withdraw money to use as you wish. But also be aware that any earnings that these accounts produce, such as interest and dividends, will be taxed at the account owner's tax rate. If you have the account in your name, you will receive a Form 1099 each year stating any dividends, interest, or other gains the investment has made. You must include these earnings on your Form 1040 when you prepare your federal and state tax returns for that year.

529/college savings plan

Savings can also be done in a specialized account earmarked for college use only. This is called a "529/college savings plan" account. (The number 529 is the Internal Revenue Code designation for this type of account.) Earnings in this account grow tax-free while you save money. You, as the parent or grandparent, control the account. A professional manages the investments in the account and makes the decisions regarding how many shares of what companies to buy for the plan.

One big advantage of a 529 account is that there are no income limitations. This simply means that no matter how much money you make each year, you can open this type of account for kids or grandkids. Money invested in this account can be paid for tuition to any college in the United States, which gives the student a lot of choices about where to attend.

Prepaid tuition account

Individual states also have their own version of the college savings plan such as Michael and Ava selected. This type of account is called a "prepaid tuition account." The account does exactly what its name implies. Anyone can contribute to this account and make either a one-time, lump-sum payment or pay in monthly installments. The advantage of this type of account is that the costs of tuition and fees are "frozen" at the time you sign up. This means that the state has calculated the amount that must be paid for tuition and fees in the future; regardless of how much these costs increase, you won't pay any more than you did when you signed up for the program.

An example is that you pay $16,000 now for your 1-year-old child to attend a state college for four years. When your 1-year-old reaches age 18, if the cost has risen to $25,000, you do not pay the increased costs. There are various options to the program regarding whether you want to prepay for a two-year community college or a four-year program. Also, the account value can be transferred to any private college or even a college that is not in your state. The amount paid also depends on the age of the child at the time you signed up for this program. The amount required for a 2-year-old would be less than for a 14-year-old because the state would have longer to invest the required payment.

Prepaid tuition programs are a great way to ensure that your child has the money needed when he or she is ready to enter college.

Loans

Although the preferred methods of financing a college education are either saving and investing before college or pay-as-you-go while attending, it is very common for students and parents to use loans to finance some of the costs. In fact, loans make up about 70 percent of financial aid. You need to know about many different types of loans, and each loan has its own requirements and conditions.

A common loan that many people use to finance college costs is a home equity loan. If your home is worth $100,000 and you owe $60,000 on your mortgage, then you have $40,000 in equity. You may borrow against the $40,000 equity and then make monthly payments to repay the home equity loan, the same as you do with your mortgage. Home equity loans are usually quick and convenient, making them a popular source of funds.

The federal government offers to lend money for college expenses through three basic loan programs: the Stafford Loan, the PLUS loan, and the Perkins Loan. The Sallie Mae Association packages loans for students, and your local bank may also provide a loan.

Stafford Loan

The Stafford Loan is a low-interest loan available for students enrolled in an undergraduate or four-year degree program. The maximum amount that you can borrow is $2,625 in the freshman year, $3,500 in the sophomore year, and $5,500 in both the junior and senior years, with a limit of $23,000 on the total loan amount. You are charged interest at a rate that can vary but is capped at 8.25 percent.

One of the great things about the Stafford Loan is that repayment doesn't begin until six months after college graduation. The loan is usually repaid over 10 years. You do need to be aware that there are two types of Stafford Loans: subsidized and unsubsidized. If the loan is subsidized, the government pays the loan interest while the student is attending college. If the loan is unsubsidized, the student is required to pay the interest. This may make a big difference in meeting monthly expenses while attending college.

PLUS

The PLUS, or Parent's Loan for Undergraduate Students, is a program that enables parents of a college student to borrow up to the total yearly costs of college for their child. Any other sources of financial aid are deducted from the amount of the PLUS loan, which a parent can borrow each year. As with other loans, the interest rate varies, but the PLUS is capped at 9 percent. Repayment begins the first month after the first check is issued. Interest begins to accumulate immediately after the loan is activated.

Perkins Loan

A loan available only to the neediest of students is the Perkins Loan. The interest rate is capped at 5 percent, which is almost half that of other loan programs. The Perkins Loan is federally subsidized, which means that interest on the loan is deferred until nine months after graduation. Students may receive up to $3,000 for the first two years, with a total loan amount available at $15,000 throughout undergraduate school.

SLMA

Sallie Mae, or the Student Loan Marketing Association (SLMA), buys student loans from many lenders. SLMA then packages loans so that repayment is affordable. One of its best programs is called the Smart Loan account, which allows students to combine all of their student loans into one account. Consolidating several loans, each with a different interest rate, allows students to reduce their monthly loan payments. Students may take up to 30 years to repay their loan amount.

Graduates may pay only the interest for two to four years. SLMA also offers the Graduated Repayment Option, which lets borrowers make small monthly payments when they have just graduated. The payments are then increased when the graduate's income increases, but the interest rate stays the same.

Private lenders

Finally, money for college expenses may be borrowed from private lenders such as your local bank. Many banks have loans designed especially for college expenses. These loans may have rates competitive with the federal loan programs offered. Usually, though, bank rates are higher because banks, as opposed to the federal government, are in business to make a profit.

The key consideration to keep in mind when borrowing is that all loans must be repaid. If possible, loan repayment should be done in the shortest amount of time possible because stretching out the payment period increases the amount of interest that must be repaid. Also, make sure that any money borrowed is used only for costs directly related to college. This is not a time to splurge—conserve any loan money, and use it wisely.

FAFSA

Using student loans is a portion of the journey that turns the dream of a college degree into reality, but the road map requires that you travel through the college student loan application process. You may have heard that completing student loan applications is a nightmare. That may be true for those who are unorganized and unprepared, but because you will be neither, completing the paperwork won't be too bad.

The form used to apply for any federal financial assistance program is the "Free Application for Federal Student Aid," or FAFSA, form. This form is used to determine eligibility for the federal student loans discussed previously. All of the information that is submitted with the form is analyzed to determine how much money per year the student and his or her family are expected to contribute toward college expenses. The information that must be supplied on this form is very detailed and includes the following:

- ❖ Yearly income from all sources for both the parents and the student (custodial parent only, if the parents are divorced)

- ❖ Total of all liabilities or debt payments
- ❖ A listing of all assets (autos, retirement accounts, and home equity are not included)
- ❖ Number of family members, especially any persons already attending college
- ❖ Federal, state, and local income tax returns
- ❖ W-2s showing yearly gross income
- ❖ Business records

All of this information is combined to compute an amount called the Expected Family Contribution (EFC). Colleges use the EFC in preparing their scholarship, grant, and other financial aid offers. As an example, if the total yearly college costs are $10,000 and the EFC is $4,000, then the remaining $6,000 may be paid through scholarships, grants, loans, and work/study, or maybe a combination of several of these methods.

The expected family contribution is computed using a process called "federal methodology." The EFC is the sum of four separate calculations:

Parent's income (custodial parent only, if divorced)

Parent's assets—5.6 percent of total assets per year

Student's income—50 percent above $2,200 per year

Student's assets—35 percent per year

The EFC analysis is very complex, and I suggest that any parent of a high school student do research in an attempt to understand the process. A great many books available at your local library explain EFC calculations. The EFC will vary depending on how many children in a family are attending college at the same time. If two children in the same household are attending, then the EFC is divided in half. If three children are attending, the expected contribution is one third.

The FAFSA cannot be submitted before January 1 of the child's senior year. I strongly suggest that you complete the form and have the necessary information available to send immediately at the first of the new calendar year. Colleges award financial aid on a "first come, first served" basis. Therefore, if you wait to complete and submit the FAFSA form, your child may receive little or no funds.

College Scholarship Service (CSS) PROFILE

The PROFILE is an additional financial aid application that some colleges and universities use to award their own scholarships, grants, and other financial aid. This a non-federal program and can be used in tandem with FAFSA. This form uses the "institutional methodology" which are formulas used by many colleges, universities, graduate and professional schools, and private scholarship programs to determine an applicant's need and eligibility for their own private, nonfederal student aid funds. This method differs from the FAFSA form in several ways. First, the income of both parents, even if divorced, is included in the calculation. Also, home equity is included in the amount of the parents' assets.

"Free Money" (or Financial Aid Funds That You Don't Have to Repay)

Free money doesn't have to be repaid. Everyone always hears about the scholarships and grants that are never awarded because no one applies for them. It's true that a tremendous amount of funds are offered by organizations. You just have to investigate any likely sources and do your homework. It's like mining for gold—it requires preparation and sometimes perspiration, but the nuggets that you find can add up to a real treasure.

Numerous sources of free financial aid are available if the applicant qualifies. Many local town organizations such as churches, Lions Clubs, Rotary Clubs, business and professional women's organizations, Chambers of Commerce, and civic organizations award scholarships to college-bound students. It is definitely worth your time and energy to find out which funds are available and to determine whether your child meets the criteria.

An employer is a good source of funds, especially if the courses completed are related to work. A surveying company may pay an employee's tuition for math courses just as an engineering company may for computer training courses. Employers see this as an investment in the employee and the company, and it's smart business.

The federal government offers "free money" college tuition in several forms.

The Pell Grant Program offers money to financially needy students with an EFC of $2,140 or less. Students must be enrolled in an undergraduate or certificate program, and a new application must be submitted every year that the student is attending college. The maximum amount of funds available from a Pell Grant varies each year but is capped at $3,125 per year per student.

The Reserve Officer Training Corps (ROTC) Scholarship Program is open to students who are ages 17 to 21 and meet certain requirements. The students must be U.S. citizens, take military science as a required subject, attend summer training, and agree to serve four years of active duty and two years of reserve duty after college graduation. ROTC scholarships pay 80 percent, or up to $8,000, per year for tuition, books, and other costs. This scholarship also provides for students to receive a monthly amount to be used for living expenses. Most colleges and universities participate in this program.

The Montgomery GI Bill is one veteran's program available to all active duty personnel who joined the military after June 30, 1985. After the serviceperson has been on duty for two years, the government contributes $275 per month to an education fund designated especially for that member. After three years, the monthly government contribution increases to $350 per month. The funds must be used for education-related expenses. Also, there are numerous programs for children of veterans, such as the AMVETS National Scholarships and the Air Force Sergeants Association Scholarship Program.

Your child or grandchild may be eligible for a National Merit Scholarship as well. This scholarship is awarded to outstanding high school students based on test scores and the student's involvement in extra activities in school. Students must qualify by taking the Preliminary Scholastic Aptitude Test/National Merit Scholarship Qualifying Test, called PSAT/NMSQT, which is taken in their junior year.

Some Room for Negotiation

The programs described here are just a few of the many sources of college financial aid. Each college or university has its own scholarships and grants, including scholarships with distinct specifications. Scholarships are available depending on the student's last name, town in which they live, age, and many other factors. The requirements for these scholarships can be so specific because they have been funded or endowed by private citizens or alumni of the college.

One last piece of important information: Most of the financial aid that is offered by individual colleges and universities is negotiable! That's right. Whatever opening offer you receive in your financial aid award letter, it is usually just that—an *opening* offer. If a particular college really wants your child, many times it will increase the amount of scholarship or grant money being offered.

Donna's Story (My Sister)

Donna's daughter, Michelle, received the highest test scores in her high school class on the Scholastic Aptitude Test (SAT). As a result, a college in a neighboring state offered her a scholarship of $4,000 per year. Michelle really wanted to attend, but because the yearly cost of tuition, books, fees, and room and board was about $16,000, it just wasn't financially practical.

Donna called the college and told them that Michelle would not be able to attend because it was not affordable. Then she negotiated additional financial aid of $4,000. With scholarship and grant money totaling $8,000 per year, Michelle was able to attend the college of her choice. This might not have happened if Donna hadn't made the phone call.

The truth is that if several colleges have accepted your child, you can contact the schools and let them know that there are competing financial aid offers. Sometimes the colleges will get into a "bidding war" by increasing the amounts they offer. Keep in mind that your child must have an outstanding academic record or have a special skill for this to work. But it's a tactic you can use when trying to get the best possible financial aid package for your child.

The bottom line is that you have to prepare and motivate your children to earn the highest grades in high school, or encourage them to develop an athletic skill if they show interest and desire. You also must do lots of homework by preparing your FAFSA form and submitting it immediately on January 1 of your child's senior year. If possible, you should visit the colleges that your child is interested in attending, and talk with school officials so that they know you and your child.

Successfully financing a college education for you, your child, or your grandchild is possible. But it takes "doing your homework" and hard work and persistence to make it happen.

Financial Aid Checklist

Doing your homework requires completing a number of action steps to make sure that you are organized and prepared. The following checklist summarizes what you just learned about applying for financial aid and will help you apply for aid from any source:

❑ Learn about all possible sources of financial aid, and develop a plan as early as possible. Request a meeting with your child's high school guidance counselor. The high school that your child attends can be a great source of information and help.

❑ Investigate every source. Scour your local phone directory and newspaper for names of organizations that could possibly offer scholarships and grants.

❑ Request college admission and financial aid information. This should be done in the fall of your child's senior year in high school, at the latest.

❑ Complete all applications accurately and legibly, and double-check the application before submitting. Incomplete applications will require a follow-up letter from the school and will delay the processing of your application.

❑ Mail admission and aid applications before the deadline. Remember, the early bird gets the worm, and the early parent gets financial aid for a child.

❑ Respond promptly to requests for additional information, and keep copies of any documents that you submit. Sometimes applications do get lost in the mail. If this happens, you must be ready to resubmit as quickly as possible.

Tax Benefits

The United States government offers tax incentives, in the form of tax credits and deductions, to parents and families who have children attending college. Many times you can have a combination of these, which will help reduce your federal taxes and thereby put more cash into your pocket.

Hope Credit

The Hope Credit is a credit against the amount of federal income tax that you will pay in a given year. The maximum amount of the credit is $1,500 per year for the first two years that your child attends college. Keep in mind that this credit can be used against the cost of tuition and fees only. Room, board, books, and other expenses are not included.

Lifetime Learning Credit

When using this credit, you may deduct $1,000 per year from the amount of payable federal income tax. After the year 2002, the credit increases to $2,000 per year. One important thing to remember is that this tax credit can be used by the entire family, not just a recent high school graduate who is attending college. Anyone may use this credit, but the maximum lifetime amount is $10,000 per family.

Tax Deductions for Student Loan Interest

Because many students must use loans to pay their college expenses, the federal government allows interest on these loans to be deducted for tax purposes. The amount deducted will increase from $2,000 in the year 2000 to $2,500 per year for the year 2001 and beyond. Interest on student loans may be deducted only for the first five years after payments begin.

Education IRA

The Roth IRA, primarily an account used to save for retirement, can also be tapped to pay college expenses. Withdrawals from a Roth IRA are taxed, but there is not a 10 percent penalty if the owner of the account is under age $59^{1}/_{2}$. Of course, if the owner is over the minimum age limit, there are no penalties or interest that must be paid.

Additional Sources of Information

What you have learned about in this chapter is a summary of information about financing a college education. Each of the loans, scholarships, grants, and other financial aid mentioned has specific details that you must know before starting your college plan. Here are some other sources of information to get you started on the right track.

American Student Assistance (ASA), 1-800-999-9080

Federal Student Aid Information, 1-800-433-3243

Higher Education Information Center, 1-800-442-1171

www.savingforcollege.com

www.collegeboard.org

www.fafsa.ed.gov

www.smartmoney.com

As mentioned before, you will profit the most by beginning at your local library. There you will find some great books that will serve as step-by-step guides through this process. Many parents and grandparents are overwhelmed at the beginning of the college planning process. That's why you must start early, even if you haven't saved a penny. Don't let the lack of money stop you. If this is your situation, you are not alone. Success requires that you become educated and develop a game plan. You, as parent or grandparent, are the captain of the team. Your team includes not only you, but also your child or grandchild, high school guidance counselor, investment adviser, accountant, and college financial aid personnel.

But make no mistake: You are the captain and must assume most of the responsibility. With persistence and help, you can reach your goal.

The Bottom Line

Education is not a luxury that you or your children can afford to do without. Fortunately, with planning, you won't have to do without it.

Reader's Journal:

Knowledge Gained:

_____

_____

_____

_____

_____

_____

_____

_____

_____

_____

Steps I Will Take:

_____

_____

_____

_____

_____

_____

_____

_____

_____

_____

Deirdre watched the annual enrollment period for the retirement plan at her company expire yet another year. She had read the plan but had unanswered questions that she was embarrassed to ask the representatives because she was a supervisor in her department. Her incomplete understanding led to some fears about enrollment. For example, she was concerned that if she contributed to the plan and then changed jobs, she would lose the amount that she had invested. When she found the courage to ask another supervisor to orient her to the retirement plan, her fears were relieved, and she enrolled.

Ten years later, Deirdre is pleased with the value of her 401(k) investments. Once she took the first step into investing, she paid attention to network news about the stock market, subscribed to a financial magazine, and adopted a favorite Internet site. She even made it her home page. Deirdre was upset about all the time she had lost in the market by not enrolling sooner, so she began contributing to an individual retirement account (IRA) at a mutual fund company that she learned about in the financial magazine.

Now, Deirdre sits down with all new hires and helps them enroll in the plan immediately. Her story motivates them to make their own commitment to participate. Management has taken note of her passion about participation in the retirement plan and often asks her to make presentations to employees. Looking back, she now says, "What was I afraid of?"

Chapter 15

Getting Started

The Bottom Line

A journey of a thousand miles begins with a single step.

—Confucius

Once Deirdre stepped into the investment waters, so to speak, she became an active swimmer. I don't know where you are in your investment steps, but taking the next one is a good idea, even if you're already investing.

What's Next?

So, what's your next step? If necessary, refer back to Chapter 2, "Here You Are," and see where you are. Then prioritize your next three steps using the following list, which outlines a number of steps in no particular sequence:

- ❏ Enroll in my company's retirement plan.
- ❏ Maximize my contribution to the company retirement plan.
- ❏ Invest in an IRA.
- ❏ Instruct my company to automatically withdraw monthly contributions to either a money market account or fund, a mutual fund, or a retirement product.
- ❏ Begin asking people who they use as an adviser.
- ❏ Set up appointments with potential advisers.
- ❏ Set up an appointment with my existing adviser to review my plan based on what I now know.
- ❏ Add an adviser to my team (accountant, stockbroker, planner, insurance agent, financial counselor).
- ❏ Invest in an individual stock.
- ❏ Make an investment transaction online.
- ❏ Visit financial Web sites to learn and search for my favorites.
- ❏ Subscribe to a financial magazine or newspaper.
- ❏ Begin talking about investing with at least one person who knows more about it than I do.
- ❏ Talk about what I've learned about investing to the women and girls in my family.
- ❏ Join or form an investment club.
- ❏ Buy an IRA for my daughter or son.
- ❏ Improve the way I talk about money with my partner.
- ❏ Look closely at my/our current investments and be sure that they are the best products for my/our needs.
- ❏ Think more seriously about what I want my life plan to be.
- ❏ Write down my life plan and calculate what I will need to fund it.
- ❏ Visit www.morningstar.com to research mutual funds.
- ❏ Visit www.financialengines.com to make sure that my investments can support my life plans (there is a small charge for the service).

❑ Hang or display a piece of art that represents my new intention to be money-smart and that quietly reinforces my commitment to financial responsibility.

❑ Note thoughts or behaviors that block my financial advancement, and get them resolved.

❑ Scrutinize my spending to uncover more money to invest or save.

❑ Other: _____

Money Therapy

Getting started means different things to different women. For some, it means learning more about investing. For others, it may be taking the action step of actually investing some money in a way that makes sense for your unique life situation. It may mean consulting a financial adviser or other money professional.

Olivia Mellan

One Step Away

You are just one step away from your next level of investment savvy. Nike says, "Just do it," and that's good advice. When reasons for not moving forward eat at your resolve, you may want to add, "Do it anyway."

The next section describes the advantages and benefits of various investment products. Most of them are available to you now, depending on your employment, your company's benefits, and your existing investment portfolio. Use this section to review your choices and to seal your understanding of each.

Individual Retirement Accounts

If you are not employed, or if your company does not have an employer-sponsored plan, you will want to invest in your own individual retirement account (IRA). There are three types of IRAs and which one you decide to contribute to depends on your situation.

Traditional IRA

You can contribute up to $2,000 a year if you have earned income. Nonworking spouses can also contribute $2,000 a year. This is a great retirement savings vehicle for women out of the workforce. Whatever you decide to invest in can grow tax-deferred. You can start withdrawing after age 59½ and must begin by age 70¹/2. If your adjusted gross income is less than $30,000 for single filers or $50,000 for joint filers you may be able to deduct the amount of the contribution from your income. Investing the maximum amount every year can be met by making monthly contributions of $166.67. This is a great way to play catch-up on your retirement savings goals.

Roth IRA

The Roth IRA is similar to the traditional IRA in that you can contribute $2,000 a year. Unlike the traditional IRA, you can withdraw the money after 59½ tax free. In addition, after five years the principal can be withdrawn at any age without penalty. Both the traditional and Roth assess penalties on the growth of the account prior to 59¹/2.

Employer-Sponsored Plans

If you are employed and your company offers a retirement plan, you'll want to enroll in it at the highest level you can afford. If you are not able to make the maximum contribution, make it your goal to get there as soon as possible. Here's a list of advantages and benefits:

❖ Automatic deductions from your paycheck.

Advantage: What you don't see, you won't miss.

Benefit: Contributions are tax-deductible and reduce the amount you pay in taxes.

❖ Employer match.

Advantage: Free money.

Benefit: Your retirement assets accumulate more rapidly.

❖ Choice of investment options.

Advantage: You determine how much risk you carry.

Benefit: You have flexibility and control over how your money is invested for retirement.

❖ Dollar cost averaging.

Advantage: Your money is invested periodically at different prices.

Benefit: You invest in up and down markets, and avoid buying and selling at extreme highs or lows.

❖ Automatic reinvested dividends and interest.

Advantage: You are earning more dividends, and dividends compound.

Benefit: More growth of your investments.

Employee Stock Ownership Programs

An employee stock ownership program, or ESOP, is a retirement-type plan, usually covering all full-time employees, in which a trust holds stock in the employee-participant's name. After an employee leaves the company (by either quitting or retiring), she cashes in on the proceeds due her.

Many plans allow you to buy stock at a discount from the market value. In some cases, your employer may even match part of your contributions. Employers also allow you to invest money in this manner outside of your retirement account. This is an excellent method to begin investing, but it requires you to do some research. Just because a company employs you doesn't make it an excellent investment opportunity.

One word of caution: Keep the ESOP portion of your portfolio to less than 10 percent of your total portfolio. You know what they say about too many eggs in one basket.

Direct Stock Investment Programs

Some of the country's most successful investors became wealthy by investing in what they know. More than 4,000 companies offer direct stock investment programs.

Direct stock investment plans allow individual investors to buy stock directly from a company without having to use a broker. Large, established companies offer these plans. More than 50 percent of American households owned stock as of 1999, and companies are finding that it makes good business sense for customers to become shareholders by purchasing stock. A happy shareholder makes a loyal customer. Here's how these plans work:

1. The shareholder establishes an account with each individual company.

2. Investment may be a one-time purchase, or money may be withdrawn from the investor's account, and shares may be purchased monthly or quarterly.

3. Dividends and interest may be paid directly to the investor or reinvested for the purchase of additional shares.

Determining which companies offered these plans had been quite difficult in the past. There are now two very popular sites (www.netstockdirect.com and www.buyandhold.com) that have made research and establishing accounts a breeze.

Dividend Reinvestment Programs (DRIPs)

Dividend Reinvestment Programs, or DRIPs, allow you to accumulate shares in stocks by reinvesting the dividends. Instead of sending dividend checks to shareholders, the company reinvests those dividends by purchasing additional shares (or fractional shares) in the shareholder's name. A shareholder usually needs only one share to enroll in the plan.

DRIPS are a great way for you to get started, especially if you want to begin with smaller amounts. Here are some of the benefits of investing in a DRIP program:

1. Involve very low fees to participate
2. Are offered by large companies
3. Allow you to participate if you already own shares of stock, or you can start a new account
4. Allow you to set up additional investments on a schedule, or whenever you have extra cash to invest
5. Use dollar cost averaging
6. Involve each company keeping track of how many shares each investor owns

Olivia Mellan

Money Therapy

All of us busy women have difficulties finding time for everything in our lives, and creating a balanced life in the process. But once we recognize how important it is to deal with our money and to make it grow and work well for us, finding some time weekly, and even a few minutes every day or so, is not that difficult. It's a question of getting it "on our radar screen" and keeping it as a priority.

The Internet has made investing using DRIPs a breeze. You can research companies and sign up online. Here are three Web sites that will help you get started:

www.investorama.com/dripcentral

www.oneshare.com

www.enrolldirect.com

Automatic Account Builders

Even though the average mutual fund requires a deposit of $2,500 to open an account, more companies are permitting initial investments of $25 to $100 if you agree to automatic withdrawal.

You complete an application, read the fund's prospectus, and write out the check. This is a great way for children to get started investing or to save for goals such as college. The Web site www.netstockdirect.com can give you access to thousands of mutual funds that offer these programs.

Most brokerage firms offer this service as well. After establishing an account, you can instruct the brokerage to automatically buy new shares of each stock on a monthly or quarterly basis.

Online Investing

The Internet has eliminated the barriers to investing. The major concern that most people have is the security issue—"Is my money safe?" You do need to make sure you're investing with reputable companies. You should feel confident that most of the investment companies that you're familiar with also have an online presence. If you want to check out these companies' ratings, go to www.gomez.com.

Many of the women in the chapter-opening stories felt uncomfortable establishing a relationship with an investment professional. Investing online eliminates the middleman. It does, however, require you to do your homework. We've mentioned several Web sites that will help you conduct research and set up an investment account online. The next sections give you a few more that are excellent at helping investors make their first move.

Coaching Tip

When you invest online, it's important to know what you're doing. A simple click can bring you rewards or disaster. Learn the computer. Learn the ins and outs of the Web site. Learn about the stock market.

Money portals

Money portals are one-stop shops for all your financial needs online. Most will allow you to conduct research, invest, and monitor your portfolio all in one place.

1. www.quicken.com
2. www.yahoofinance.com
3. www.msn.moneycentral.com
4. www.Bloomberg.com
5. www.cbsmarketwatch.com
6. www.smartmoney.com
7. www.financialmuse.com

Investment company sites

Many of the large investment companies have transformed their Web sites into portals as well. Remember, these companies also sell their proprietary products.

www.fidelity.com

www.vanguard.com

www.schwab.com

www.troweprice.com

One of the other benefits to online trading is the ability to track your investments online. Most allow you to make your own home page and track your investment portfolio. No more looking at your statements every quarter and trying to crunch the numbers. You can have everything in one place.

Investment Clubs

Women are starting investment clubs in droves. It's fun, it's social, and you can learn how to make money in the process. The National

Association of Investors Corporation, or NAIC, is the organization that has been responsible for helping groups establish investment clubs. The number of investment clubs has tripled since 1993, as interest in the stock market has increased.

An investment club allows you to leverage the experience of several people rather than trying to go it alone. However, keep in mind that just getting a group of people together does not guarantee success.

Here are the key areas you need to consider to get your investment club started through the NAIC (or, you may want to form one on your own):

1. **Get general information.** The NAIC provides you with a video that shows a meeting of a well-run club and has local councils in more than a hundred cities that meet once a month. The NAIC has recently introduced a "model club." You and your members attend a meeting of an investment club that is already up and running to serve as the template and resource for you and your members.

2. **Choose members.** Probably the best advice I can give is to find someone with a general working knowledge of investments to be the president or managing partner of your club. This can save you a tremendous amount of time because some members may need to ask questions, and a somewhat experienced person will probably fit the bill. You are looking for potential members with not only desire, but also commitment. Some people will want to join because of the social aspect but won't be willing to do investment research and be active participants. Your goal should be to find people who want to contribute and learn along the way. Go for quality over quantity. You'll need a minimum of five people to delegate the responsibilities needed to run a club.

3. **Choose an operating structure.** Now you have to give your club a name. Sounds easy enough, but remember that once you name the club, it must become a legal entity and must be formed as a corporation or a partnership. I suggest that you get some professional assistance. Your accountant or attorney can help you establish the organization and advise you of the tax implications of your decision. *This is the most important step.* You can do it on your own, but make sure that everyone involved understands the ramifications of their decision. Probably the least understood step

in forming an investment club is whether you should organize as a partnership or a corporation.

4. **Elect your officers.** Every organization must have officers to fulfill roles. Your officers' titles are less important than the actual work they have to do. Make sure that the responsibilities of each role are explained to your members. This will help them determine whether they can fulfill the responsibilities. The president or presiding partner, secretary, treasurer, and financial partner are the most important components. If the right people are chosen to begin with, you'll start with a solid foundation. The organizational structure will help to accomplish your ultimate goal of creating wealth as a group.

5. **Conduct meetings.** This is the fuel needed for your club to become successful. Initially your meeting will act as a classroom where you gain the knowledge needed to make investments. By analyzing potential investments for the club, members learn how to make investment decisions. Many clubs take a haphazard approach and don't devote time and energy to the decision-making process. You can use these same skills to create your own investment portfolio.

6. **Track performance.** The progress and performance of your investment portfolio need to be reviewed at each meeting. The often sought-after and touted "Beardstown Ladies" investment club had to reduce the rates of return quoted on their portfolios and are a testament that forming an investment club does not provide an overall investment education. As the Beardstown Ladies discovered, performance should be measured and accurate. The NAIC now provides software and, in some instances, local workshops to help in this area.

Several Web sites are now available that can assist you in forming investment clubs:

www.investorama.com

www.bivio.com

www.better-investing.com

You Have What You Need

You already have what you need to get started. Clean the slate today. Begin where you are. Let me know what your steps are by e-mailing me at debo@greenpurse.com. And, of course, you can always contact me with your questions and comments. The book's not over yet, though, so read on.

The Bottom Line

Every step you take makes the next one easier.

Reader's Journal:

Knowledge Gained:

_____

_____

_____

_____

_____

_____

_____

_____

_____

Steps I Will Take:

_____

_____

_____

_____

_____

_____

_____

_____

_____

Pamela was an account manager for a Big Five accounting firm. She was intrigued and often shocked by the stories of people getting wealthy overnight in the stock market. She had been to graduate school and felt that she had an adequate understanding of finance, yet investing had never held an interest for her—until now. She was determined to become a day trader and earn the kind of money she was reading about.

Pamela had little or no experience researching stocks, although her 401(k) had grown nicely over the years. In her mind, she believed that she should be able to do as well as the professional investors, and certainly as well as the amateur investors she was reading about in the media. She prepared to dive into investing in advanced ways. Pamela's husband, alarmed at what she was about to do, referred her to me.

I asked Pamela what her existing portfolio looked like and how much experience she had investing. "I have my 401(k) and some savings, and that's about it," Pamela said. "I have never invested in stocks." I asked Pamela if she had ever been to Las Vegas. She laughed and said, "No, I'm not a gambler." I said, "If you decide to day trade, that's exactly what you'll be doing, because 9 out of 10 people lose money on day trading."

What Pamela didn't understand is that you need to have earned the right to be a high-risk, advanced investor. She was not even close. Most people, including experienced investors like me, never are—and don't want to be.

Chapter 16

Advanced Investing

The Bottom Line
High-risk, advanced investment products put your money in jeopardy.

I want you to be knowledgeable about the entire range of investment products—even the advanced products presented in this
chapter, which most people, including me, never use in their
entire investment experience. Keep in mind that I am not recommending these advanced tools, only making you aware of them.

By "advanced," I mean more risky products. Someone will likely
try to get you to buy into at least one or more of these "opportunities." By reading this chapter, you'll be able to identify them
when they come your way.

Some friends, mostly brokers, and I were sitting around the table recently, talking about high-risk investing. Our voices were becoming animated, we were starting to gulp water, and some of us were getting out of our seats. A woman in the group who was not a broker said, "Wow, talking about high-risk products is getting you guys really excited. What's the deal?" She was right. Like kids talking ghost stories around the campfire, we were getting ourselves worked up. We each had our tale to tell and few, if any, of them turned out well.

"What percentage of your clients use these advanced tools?" she wondered.

"Maybe 2 percent," I answered. The other brokers agreed.

Then she asked, "Do any of you use them?" Unanimously, we said "No." Like a parent admitting to smoking pot in college, I confessed to investing in high-risk stocks when I first got into the business. I lost all the money I had invested. "It woke me up really fast," I said.

She asked, "Then why in the world would you devote a chapter in your book to something so dangerous?"

I said, "Because I want the reader to be prepared. I want her to be able to know the language and recognize the products when someone mentions them." Someone somewhere will try to get you to invest in a high-risk product. You'll be told a great story about nearly instant wealth, and you'll be tempted. I say go ahead and be tempted, but unless you set aside a small amount to "play" with as you would in Las Vegas, you should resist the urge to gamble your money in this way.

Caution!

Before you consider using any one of the investment tools discussed in this chapter, you must take the following steps:

1. Have your financial plan in place.
2. Be participating fully in your 401(k) plan.
3. Be completely funding your IRA.
4. Have your 6 to 12 months' worth of cash reserves saved.
5. Be able to walk away from whatever money you commit to these strategies and lose it all.
6. Be able to lose it all without having that loss destroy your overall financial plan.

Get Rich Quick? Not Likely

You've seen the advertisements on late-night television—offers to trade options and futures like the big institutions and make big money in the process. Funny how they don't mention the risks.

This isn't to say that investors don't use these strategies every day. They do. And every day they lose and, yes, sometimes win. More often than not, however, such strategies are nothing more than glorified get-rich-quick schemes. As advanced as these skills are, the risks associated with them increase as well. Just because you take more risk doesn't mean that you automatically make more money. You very well may lose money. If you aren't willing to live by those rules, then these strategies aren't for you.

So here we go. Let's meet some highly aggressive, advanced investment strategies.

Margin Accounts

Simply put, buying on "margin" is the right to borrow against the stocks, bonds, and mutual funds in your portfolio. You can use that borrowing power to buy stocks for which you don't have enough cash, to short stocks (see the "Shorting" section later in this chapter), or to participate in very aggressive strategies such as options and futures. In its simplest terms, buying on margin allows investors to get more bang for their buck. But be aware that the bigger "bang" can also blow up in your face.

Not all securities are marginable, particularly those that are less than 30 days old, such as IPOs and newly purchased mutual fund shares. Always check with your adviser to see if the one you're considering qualifies.

There is currently a Securities and Exchange Commission (SEC) requirement, called Regulation T, that you can borrow no more than 50¢ for every dollar of stock you buy. Let's say that you deposit $1,000 into a brokerage account, and you want to buy $1,500 worth of a certain stock (100 shares at $15 each). (We'll disregard transaction costs for this example.) You have $1,000 of equity in the position, and you owe $500 to the firm, from which you borrowed the additional cash to make the purchase. (And remember, the firm will charge you interest on this margin balance. It won't lend you money for free.) Your margined percentage is $500 ÷ $1,500 = 33 percent. That meets the Regulation T requirement of no more than 50 percent borrowed money at the time of purchase.

There is also an SEC maintenance requirement of 25 percent equity, or no more than 75 percent borrowed money. This allows the price of the margined stock to fluctuate, as it will on a daily basis.

Let's say that the stock drops to $5 per share. That means that your position is now worth $500 (100 shares × $5 per share). Your margin balance is still $500. So, $500 margin balance ÷ $500 stock value = 100 percent. You now have more than 75 percent borrowed money, which triggers a "margin call." This means that the firm holding your account requires you to deposit additional cash or stock to meet the margin maintenance requirement. How much? If the stock is worth $500, you must maintain 25 percent equity, or $125. So, you would have to write a check for $125 to maintain the position. If you don't, the firm can sell as much of the stock as it needs to in order to meet the margin requirement, and it doesn't have to get your permission to do it. If the stock continues to drop, you must continue to deposit additional cash to meet the margin maintenance requirements.

Different firms have higher maintenance requirements than the SEC's 25 percent number. With the way the prices of many stocks bounce around, most notably technology stocks, a lot of firms won't let you borrow against these stocks at all. Be sure to check with your firm to see what its specific requirements are.

Shorting

Making money in stocks is often described as "buy low, sell high." You can also do this in reverse—"sell high, buy low." This is known as "shorting" or "selling short."

Here's how it works. You borrow stock from the firm, sell it, and buy it back later, hopefully at a lower price. But to do this, you must have margin privileges in place. And shorting stocks is subject to the same Regulation T requirements as buying stocks. But because you're shorting, it's 100 percent plus the Regulation T 50 percent, so you need to have 150 percent of the current value of the stock in cash to start.

Let's say that you shorted or sold 100 shares of a $15 stock. That means you sold the stock and took in $1,500. You will have to put in

$750 more in cash to meet the margin requirement. If the stock drops in price to $10, as you expect, you then buy the stock back for $1,000 and you have made a $500 profit. But if the stock goes up in price to $25 and it's now valued at $2,500 you would have lost a thousand dollars.

Coaching Tip

When you get your brokerage statement, you will see you own a stock either long or short. If you are "long" the stock, you own it outright. If you are "short" the stock, you have borrowed it and sold it. Look at your statements.

Futures

Futures are used to buy a particular commodity such as corn, coffee, or pork bellies at some point in the future at today's price by a particular date. For example, let's say you believe that wheat prices are going to rise. You can purchase a futures option giving you the right to buy bushels at today's price six months later. Of course the longer the time frame to the future represents, the more it costs or the higher the premium is. All futures contracts expire on the third Saturday of a given month. So, the last day to trade them is the Friday before. At the expiration date, you must be prepared to either take physical delivery or purchase a contract that closes out the position.

It used to be that most futures were used in association with agriculture-related commodities—things such as coffee, cocoa, cotton, and pork bellies. Now, most of the futures that are traded are financially oriented, such as currencies and market indexes. Futures are most often used by large companies with big proportions of their expenses tied to one thing. For example, a huge part of an airline's expenses come from fuel costs, so many airlines engage in futures trading (and futures options) to control their fuel costs.

Buying futures is also subject to margin requirements. But the most important thing to know about futures is that, because they are highly leveraged by their very structure, you can lose more than you put in. Also, don't overlook the issue of physical delivery. In the example of the airline, it may actually want to take delivery of several thousand gallons of jet fuel. It would certainly be better equipped to handle that delivery than the ordinary investor. Are you prepared to have a tractor trailer back up to your garage and unload several tons of corn or pork bellies? My freezer isn't big enough to hold all that!

Options

Options are the right to buy or sell a particular stock at a particular price (called the strike price) by a particular date (the expiration date). Selling is sometimes referred to as writing an option. Like futures, options expire on the third Saturday of a given month, so the last day to trade those options is the Friday before.

Coaching Tip

Options trade like stocks. They have their own price. You don't own the stock, you own the option.

Puts and Calls

There are two types of options: puts and calls. Puts are the right to sell your stock to someone at the strike price by the expiration date. Calls are the right to buy stock from someone at the strike price by the expiration date.

The price of an option is called a "premium." One option covers 100 shares of stock. So, let's say that the option you're considering buying sells for $3. If you buy one option contract, it will cost you a premium of $300 (ignoring transaction costs). If you buy 10 contracts, that covers 1,000 shares (10 × 100 shares), and the premium is $3,000.

If you want to buy a call on XYZ stock, it will be identified like this: XYZ June 30s. This means that if you buy this call, you will have the right to buy XYZ at $30 per share until the June expiration date. Part of the price of the option will be based on the difference between the stock price and the strike price. There will also be a part of the price that reflects that the option won't expire until sometime in the future. If you buy the call, you're saying that you expect XYZ to go up in price. If you're wrong, the most you will lose is the amount that you invested. If you're right, and the stock increases in price, your option will increase in value and you can sell at a profit.

Puts and calls can be done "covered" or "naked." Covered refers to the fact that you already own the stock. Naked means you don't own it.

Covered Call

The most often used and least aggressive of the option strategies is the covered call. In this case, you own XYZ and sell a call against that stock. This means that you're willing to part with your stock at the strike price, and if it stays below the strike price, you're willing to hold on to it. As the seller, you pocket the premium and hope that the stock is below the strike price when the option expires. That way, you keep both the premium and the stock. The worst that can happen with a covered call is that you get the premium and lose the stock. You have to sell the stock because it "got called away from you."

Naked Call

Let's look at the opposite scenario—selling a naked call. In this instance, you sold a call against stock that you don't own. That means that if your option is exercised against you, you will be obligated to buy the stock in the open market at any price, and sell it to someone who bought that call at the strike price. So, if the price of the stock goes up dramatically, you could lose a significant amount of money because you don't own the stock.

For example, say that you sold one naked call contract for XYZ June 30s. Time passes, and it is now just before the expiration date. XYZ is at $100 per share. Because you sold the call naked, you have to go out into the market and buy XYZ at $100, and have the call exercised at $30. So, you're out $100 – $30 × 100 = $7,000. And that's just *one* contract! As you can see, the worst-case scenario can be pretty terrible.

Now look at puts. If you buy a put, then you're expecting the stock to go down. If it doesn't, then at worst you've lost what you spent to buy the put. If the stock does drop, then your put goes up in value.

If you sell a put, then you have the right to buy someone's stock at a specific price. By selling a put, you expect that the stock will go up. When it does, then you keep the premium, and the put expires, worthless. If the stock goes down, then you need to have the cash to pay for the stock, which may be worth much less in the marketplace than you paid.

Futures Options

Futures options are puts and calls on futures contracts. As the name implies, they are a hybrid of futures and options, and therefore they are exceedingly aggressive.

You may have heard of a "triple-witching" day on the nightly business report. That's the last day that options, futures, and futures options contracts trade before their expiration on Saturday. The markets tend to be very volatile during that week, and particularly on that Friday, as traders scramble to prepare for their positions to expire, get called for exercise, or be delivered. In other words, they now have to deliver the securities they gave someone the right to buy or sell from them.

Index Options

Index options represent a specific index and not an individual security. For example, you can purchase an option on the S&P 500 Index which represents 500 different stocks. Like stock options there are calls and puts. You purchase the options based on whether you think the overall market will go up or down.

Conclusions

To reiterate—and this can't be emphasized enough—you have to earn the right to be an advanced investor. Any money that you choose to invest in products such as options and futures must be considered disposable money. Remember, the greater the risk, the greater the potential reward, but also the greater the potential loss. You must be organized and have your financial plan in place, funded and working. You have to be able to lose all of the money that you decide to invest this way, without that loss destroying your overall financial plan.

The Bottom Line

It isn't that you're more skilled if you pursue these strategies, it's that you're taking more risk.

Reader's Journal:

Knowledge Gained:

_____

_____

_____

_____

_____

_____

_____

_____

_____

_____

Steps I Will Take:

_____

_____

_____

_____

_____

_____

_____

_____

_____

_____

Leslie was comfortable making her own investment decisions. Investing had become a hobby for her right out of college. After investing in mutual funds for years, she opened a brokerage account with a broker she met at a conference. That relationship grew and she shifted some of the money that had been invested in mutual funds to individual stocks that were recommended by her broker.

Her portfolio reached the million dollar mark. Each time her broker or a representative at the investment company brought up the subject of estate planning, Leslie simply shrugged it off. But after attending a seminar on estate planning, Leslie faced reality. She didn't have children or a husband and really hadn't thought about who in her family should get what. When she learned that she might have to pay estate taxes to the tune of almost forty percent, she panicked.

She laughs at herself now but that seminar was the catalyst for her seeking the expertise she needed at this stage in her financial life. First, she called her broker to see whether her firm had any expertise in estate planning. Her broker referred her to an attorney she worked with closely. She also made an appointment with the attorney who conducted the seminar. Leslie called her accountant to inquire whether she could help explain the estate tax issues further.

After all was said and done, Leslie hired the attorney from the seminar to create a trust for her. She then had to register her investments in the name of the trust. Her reluctance had always been that she didn't want one adviser to be privy to information on her total portfolio. Her accountant was the only adviser who knew everything.

Leslie still is quite active in managing her portfolio, but she relies on her broker, attorney, and accountant for their expertise.

Chapter 17

Selecting Your Best Advisers

The Bottom Line

Select advisers who know their specialty, communicate in terms you understand, and treat you with respect.

Selecting an adviser is one of your most critical decisions. There are many advisers to choose from, and it's important to remember that *you* are hiring *them*, not the other way around.

Here's a way to find out quickly how well a financial professional communicates:

Even if you understand what's being said, ask, "What do you mean by [asset allocation]? Would you please explain that another way?"

The adviser's response will tell you a lot about the level of respect and communication that you will experience in your relationship.

Do Your Homework

The bottom line on selecting an advisory team is to do your home-work, make your selection, and stick with the people you select. There is no substitute for preparation, and because the people you select will probably be your guides for some time, you should do as much prepar-ing and interviewing as needed until you find the right fit for your sit-uation.

There's an old saying that two heads are better than one. This is espe-cially true in an area like financial services. I like the team approach. An investment adviser may be the best in her field but might not fully know or understand taxes. A CPA knows a lot about personal taxes but often knows little about insurance products that can benefit an overall financial plan. Therefore, a team of advisers, each educated and experi-enced in her own specialty, is the best approach.

Why You Need an Adviser

If you're like millions of other people, you work hard and try to save as much as possible. That's good because there will be milestones in your financial life: college for you, your children, or all of you; caring for aging parents or loved ones; a second career; and either full or par-tial retirement. But how do you successfully pass each of these mile-stones and get to where you want to be? That's right—by using an adviser. Here are some advantages of using an adviser.

Vast Number of Products

The vast number of products/investment vehicles and incredible array of mutual funds, stocks, bonds, and other investments can cause analysis paralysis if you're doing it without help. An adviser can help you navigate this minefield.

Specialized Knowledge

Sometimes you can really lose money by being a "do-it-yourselfer." Preparing your own taxes is one example. Your tax situation may be simple enough, but you may miss a new deduction or strategy. What you don't know can cost you.

Another example is insurance. Owning the right types and amounts of insurance is extremely important. Do you know if you have what you need? There are many uses of insurance besides paying a death benefit when someone dies. Insurance can be used to make investments, make up for lost wages if you are temporarily unable to work, and protect your loved ones from undue tax penalties upon your death, to name a few. An adviser provides the specialized knowledge that "do-it-your-selfers" need but don't have.

Clearer Path

An effective adviser will keep you moving on the path you've chosen. Achieving your financial milestones requires the accumulation of wealth, and that requires much preparation, thought, and follow-through. The decisions that you make and the actions that you take will make a tremendous difference in whether you reach your life goals. The right adviser can help ensure that you reach them.

Your Team

Establishing an advisory team with whom you can establish a good rapport, trust, and open discussion is something that you can do for yourself over time, if not immediately. Your team might include a financial planner, who acts as a "quarterback," a stockbroker, an accountant, an insurance agent, and an attorney.

Why a Team?

A team gives you a wide perspective on the choices you will make. Members of your financial team may even disagree on a point. The value they bring is giving you more than one way to view your choices. Ultimately, you will make the decisions, but your advisers will provide information that will help you make the best decision for each situation.

A financial advisory team has four basic jobs:

1. Create and grow wealth for you
2. Protect and preserve your wealth
3. Plan for the most tax-advantaged distribution of wealth during life
4. Plan for the most tax-advantaged distribution of wealth at death

These are your main goals, too. Creating and preserving wealth is not a quick or easy process, which is why an adviser, or team of advisers, is essential. On our own, we may skip very important steps.

Qualities of an Effective Adviser

Every good adviser must have several traits.

Trustworthiness

Trustworthiness is first because it is the foundation for your relationship with your financial adviser. All the good looks, smooth talk, and letters behind her last name on her business card don't mean much if you don't have faith in what she's telling you. Having trust and faith means having a comfortable feeling about the path you're on; not having it means questioning almost everything that your adviser recommends. Because your financial journey lasts a lifetime, be certain that you trust the adviser(s) you're bringing with you on the trip.

The Ability to Educate

A good adviser must be an educator. Most people who are good at their profession possess this trait. A good teacher communicates well and is willing to explain something more than once and in more than one way, if necessary. Remember, advisers have gone to school to learn what they know. Expect an adviser to translate terms and concepts to you in ways that you can grasp, and never be afraid to ask a question more than once.

A good financial adviser will also help you understand whatever investments you may already own. For instance, if you work for a school system, a hospital, a state government, or the federal government, you probably have a pension called a "defined benefit pension." You work for a certain number of years, and when you reach retirement age, you're paid a monthly pension for the rest of your life. This is very different from "defined contribution" accounts such as a 401(k) or a 403(b), which are retirement accounts into which you, as an employee, contribute most of the money. You can take your defined contribution pension with you if you leave your present employer. That's not so with the defined benefit pension, which is rarely transferable. Understanding the difference in investments such as these and how they all fit together to your best advantage is extremely important.

An adviser who educates you will lead you to your best solutions.

Listening Ability

Have you ever sought advice from someone who did nothing but talk? The expert told you what she thought and gave her opinion, with very little input from you. Frustrating!

One of the greatest listeners of the twentieth century was Jacqueline Kennedy. She was remarkable for her ability to focus on whoever was speaking to her, comprehend what was being discussed, and give insightful feedback. Advisers must also have this ability to listen if they're going to comprehend your needs and give you insightful advice.

You must be able to fully express your goals, fears, hopes, dreams, and present financial situation. Your adviser should listen, take notes, ask questions, and then give you feedback on what you just said. Only then can your adviser start to fully understand where you are now and where you want to go, and then formulate a plan to get you there.

Communication Skills

An effective adviser not only listens, but she also gives feedback, offering insight and clarity. An adviser in any field must translate the language and concepts to the client. In the case of a financial adviser, she will interpret the language and concepts of the financial industry, and, in terms you can understand, explain how each investment recommended will contribute to your portfolio as a whole.

A good communicator will make sure that the person listening has a working knowledge of the subject so that the best possible decisions can be made.

Objectivity

Objectivity is crucial in choosing investments. Just because a certain stock or mutual fund has performed well and is the "hot pick" of the moment doesn't mean that it's right for you. A good financial adviser keeps current on new financial products and updated on products already being sold, viewing them objectively with you in mind.

A good financial adviser also doesn't let the amount of commissions paid to her influence her suggestions about what investments will ultimately be chosen for your portfolio.

Some advisers maintain relationships with only 5 to 10 mutual funds and "plug" their clients into one of these favorites. Sometimes that's like trying to stick a square peg into a round hole—it's just not a good fit. When interviewing financial advisers, make sure to ask what products they normally choose for their clients. If you can count on one hand the number of mutual funds or stocks mentioned, it's probably a sign that the adviser is too restrictive in her selections.

Coaching Tip

Listen to your financial adviser and take her advice. If you don't agree, talk about it until you or she has a different understanding.

Competence

Competence may seem like an obvious qualification to you, but it's not always obvious that an adviser is incompetent. Just because someone says she's been a financial adviser for a period of years doesn't mean that she knows what she should know and can do her job at a high level. Sometimes it just means that she hasn't found anything else she would rather do.

The financial industry has standards that each adviser must meet. These standards help ensure that a minimum level of service is provided to each client. One of the best ways to make sure that the person you choose is competent is through professional designations.

Professional Designations

Let's talk for a minute about the "alphabet soup" of professional designations for financial professionals. Numerous sets of letters can follow a person's name on her business card; each represents a certain area or level of expertise. The following list will help you identify each one and know its meaning.

1. **RR.** This adviser is a registered representative with a brokerage house and has passed tests given by the National Association of Security Dealers. At the very minimum, an RR has a Series 6 license to sell mutual funds and has passed a test to get a state license where she does business. An RR is usually a starting point for a financial professional because no college degree, license, or certification is required.

2. **RIA.** A registered investment adviser is someone who has passed the Series 65 test and the state test where she does business. An RIA may or may not be licensed to sell investments. Usually, an RIA creates financial plans to suit the purpose of the client. RIAs may create plans that include college costs, future retirement income needs, and eldercare planning for the client or the client's family.

3. **CFP.** Certified financial planners must complete a difficult two-year course during which they are trained in insurance needs, investments, estate planning, and many other facets of investment planning. CFPs not only are able to create financial plans but, if they are licensed, they also may suggest and execute the trades necessary to buy and sell investments for their clients.

4. **CPA.** Someone who possesses this designation is a certified public accountant and is thoroughly educated and trained in all areas of taxation. You may hire a CPA each year to prepare your income taxes. CPAs also know about other areas, including taxes for small businesses, estate taxes, and capital gains taxes.

5. **CLU.** Life insurance is always a part of any financial plan, and the certified life underwriter knows how to plan for unexpected emergencies and use life insurance to protect assets. Many people think of life insurance as a policy that pays a certain amount of money when someone dies. But the many uses of life insurance go far beyond that. CLUs can suggest ways to use insurance to reduce income taxes while investing for your child's college education and your retirement, and can eliminate or reduce estate taxes that your heirs will pay after your death.

6. **PFA.** A personal financial adviser is a financial planner who has at least five years of experience in the financial planning field and has passed a series of examinations. This is a new designation that was created by the National Association of Security Dealers.

As mentioned before, impressive as it might be, a financial designation doesn't guarantee that a particular adviser will be the right one for you. It does mean that an adviser has additional education and expertise beyond what is required to simply create a financial plan or sell investments. It's also a good indication that an adviser has invested much time and effort in being knowledgeable and is dedicated to remaining in the financial services field.

Now that you know why a financial adviser is necessary and what to look for in choosing one, let's discuss how to find the right one for you.

How to Find an Adviser

The most common way to find an expert, whether it be a plumber, a lawyer, a carpenter, or a financial adviser, is to ask people who they use and whether they're pleased with the expert's knowledge and service.

If a friend or relative is happy with the service she has received, chances are good that you'll have the same positive experience. But remember that working with a financial adviser for years is different from working with someone on an occasional basis. The commitment to having a good working relationship is much greater.

A great source of information about a professional is another professional. If a CPA prepares your taxes, or if you have a family lawyer or insurance agent, or if you have gotten to know someone at your local bank, ask who they would recommend as a financial adviser. Many times professionals work with each other on an ongoing basis and get to know each other very well. Also, don't be surprised if you ask your CPA, attorney, insurance agent, or bank manager for a referral and that person suggests her own personal financial adviser. It's all about establishing long-term relationships with people you can trust.

Money Therapy

Remember, in choosing a financial planner, that you have many choices and you can interview a variety of folks until you find one with whom you feel truly comfortable. You can ask about their experience and their areas of specialization, decide whether you want a fee-only planner or not, and ask about their fee structure until you understand it fully. Perhaps most important, ask them enough questions about things you don't understand to see whether they answer you without your feeling put down or judged.

Olivia Mellan

Most professionals belong to professional associations or organizations. The Financial Planning Association (FPA) is one that many certified financial planners join. Organizations such as the FPA maintain current rosters of members and may give referrals to the general public. They also offer financial advisers continuing education on new products and developments in their field. The phone number for the FPA is 1-800-282-7526; its Web site is www.fpanet.org.

How Advisers Get Paid

Just as you wouldn't buy a car without asking how much it costs, you shouldn't select a financial adviser without asking what she charges and how she gets paid. Financial advisers perform a service for which they deserve to be compensated; it's just that compensation can come in many different ways and combinations.

Some financial professionals will give a prospective client a fact sheet that contains information such as where they graduated from college, what professional licenses they have, any specialized training courses they've taken, and the fees or commissions they charge. If the financial adviser doesn't offer this information when you interview her, ask for it. Many times the company that the adviser works for will already have a brochure or package with information about the company and how their advisers are compensated. If information about how the adviser is paid is not included in such information, ask to see the contract or application that you must complete to become a client. Information about fees, commissions, and charges must be disclosed to you before you sign a contract to become a client. Make sure you get it.

Discussed in the next sections are some ways that advisers get paid. Remember that many times advisers can receive a combination of these methods.

Salary

Most financial advisers receive some portion of their pay from a salary, a set amount that they receive every pay period. Imagine a pyramid, with salary being the bottom or base of the pyramid and fees and commissions layered above it. The base salary for advisers at most brokerage houses is modest.

Commission

A commission is money paid to a salesperson based on the value of the item sold. If an adviser sells stock worth $100 and receives a 1 percent commission, the adviser gets paid $1. You pay a commission every time you buy or sell a stock. Usually, the brokerage house or business where the investment adviser works has a commission schedule based on the number of shares that are sold. Be aware that you may pay more if you buy a smaller-than-usual number of shares of a stock or mutual fund. If you buy 1 share of a stock, the commission may be just as much as, or even greater than, if you buy 100 shares.

Your adviser may be paid what are called "trailing commissions." If you set up a "wealth builder" account, which is done by having a certain amount of your paycheck invested each month, your adviser will also be paid every time new money is invested in your account.

Another member of your advisory team, your insurance agent, is usually paid on commission as a percentage of the policy premiums that are paid during the year.

Fee-Only

In the past 10 years, a large number of financial advisers have started charging a fee and don't get paid from commissions. A fee-only planner will meet with you, collect information and statements on your present financial situation, find out your goals and plans for the future, and create a financial plan especially for you. It may be a plan for sending your child to college, or it may be more complex—not only college, but also a cruise around the world, retirement planning, eldercare planning for you and your spouse, and funding an estate.

Some advisers charge hourly fees ranging from $75 to $500 per hour. Others have standard fees, depending upon the type of plan you need. For example, a plan for funding your child's college education may be $250, and a plan that includes college and retirement may be $500.

Money Management

It's not enough just to create a plan, start investing the money, and then forget it. Good financial plans are like gardens—they need to be cared for and cultivated. Financial advisers are the gardeners. They not only create the garden, they also maintain it. This means that as your account value grows, your investment adviser must review your portfolio, weed out any investments that aren't growing well, and replace them with new ones that will thrive in that particular spot.

Financial advisers who manage accounts are usually paid a percentage of assets under management. The percentage charged varies by how much your account is worth. Fees can start at 5 percent and decrease to less than 1 percent as the size of your account increases. For example, an account that contains $5,000 may be charged 3 percent, or $150 per year. An account valued at $1,000,000 may be charged .50 percent per year, or $5,000. Certainly, $5,000 is a lot of money, but if you have a good adviser and your account grows $100,000 per year, then paying $5,000 to make $100,000 is a pretty good return.

The old saying "You get what you pay for" is usually true with financial advisers also. Don't make inexpensive money management fees the primary reason for choosing your investment adviser.

Interviewing an Adviser

You may not have had the experience of hiring someone before. Meeting with and choosing a prospective adviser is not something that should be done quickly or without preparation. During the interview, you may get a "gut" reaction about the person you're talking with, but you shouldn't jump to conclusions or make on-the-spot decisions. Ask the same questions of everyone you meet with, take notes, and then carefully make your choice.

Always interview at least three people for each type of adviser you need. This is a good rule that should not be broken. Why? Because you will learn from each person you talk with, even though you're asking the same questions. Also, each adviser you interview may be from a different company and have different methods of creating plans and different methods of getting paid for their services. You can always interview more than three, but you should never interview less.

Sample Advisor Interview Questions

Before the interview, write down a list of questions that you want your prospective adviser to answer. The following list includes sample questions that you can add to your own:

1. *What is your educational background?* Most advisers have college degrees, and some have a master of business administration (MBA) degree, but don't be too impressed by this. It's true that if someone has a master's degree, that person has learned more specialized information than someone with a bachelor's degree. Of course, the degree should be in the area of business, because an engineer usually doesn't learn about advanced investment strategies in college.

2. *What are your credentials?* In other words, what has this adviser accomplished? Has this person attended advanced financial courses to expand her job knowledge? Has she written and published books on her particular area of expertise? Has she been voted one of the 10 best planners in the city? Did someone you trust refer you to her?

3. *What is your background and experience? How long have you been an adviser? Have you worked continuously for the same firm? Do you have a working knowledge of a broad range of investment products, or have you specialized in one particular investment such as bonds?* This will give you an indication of their experience and areas of expertise.

4. *What type of clients do you advise?* An adviser may have limited the business to only commercial clients with 401(k) plans. Also, some advisers take on only "high-end" clients with $500,000 or more of assets in their accounts.

5. *What type of financial plans do you create? Are the plans for one particular event, such as retirement, or do you create plans that include saving for life events, such as college and retirement? How many pages and how many illustrations do your plans usually contain?* Your goal is to have a thorough, concise plan. A large, elaborate plan with 100 pages may be a lot of "fluff." Make sure that you get and pay for only what you really need.

6. *How often do you meet with clients?* It's important for you to know how often the adviser reviews client accounts. Many advisers review their clients' accounts daily just to see how certain investments are performing. They don't change investments; they just keep an eye on things. Periodic meetings with clients keep an adviser informed of any events in the client's life, such as the birth of a child, which may affect how a portfolio is invested. Periodic meetings also keep you, the client, educated on how your account is growing and keep you involved in the wealth-building process.

7. *How are you compensated?* The discussion earlier in this chapter will give you a good basis for understanding how each particular adviser may get paid. You must decide whether you want a fee-only adviser who will create your plan but let you make the investments, or whether you want someone to "tend your garden" and have an active involvement in building your wealth.

8. *Do you have any current clients that I could talk to?* This goes back to the information on referrals. Talking with current clients is a great way of finding out how an adviser performs the job. You can even ask an adviser's current client some of the questions that were just discussed. Usually, happy customers are willing to let others know about the great service they receive. A current client could be your most valuable source.

Go!

Are you ready to seek an adviser? Remember, you are the one hiring the adviser, so you get to decide who to hire according to your own criteria. Let this be a confidence-building experience and one that keeps you in the driver's seat.

The Bottom Line

A good investment adviser will partner with you, not dominate or overrule you. Choose someone whose skill you trust, whose manner makes you comfortable, and whose knowledge is always on the rise.

Reader's Journal:

Knowledge Gained:

_____

_____

_____

_____

_____

_____

_____

_____

_____

Steps I Will Take:

_____

_____

_____

_____

_____

_____

_____

_____

_____

Charlene has just graduated from college and landed an advertising job. She's happy to be earning $30,000 a year and not having to worry about the next exam. She has a student loan of $10,000 to pay off and has determined that her first purchase will be a brand new Passat. Charlene knows that she needs to save and invest. Her company offers a retirement plan and will match 50¢ on the dollar, up to 6 percent of her salary. The company also has an employee stock option program that would allow Charlene to purchase stock at a discount. If she decides to participate in the plan, she won't be able to afford the new car payment or pay off her student loan. If you were Charlene, what would you do?

Rhonda is 44 years old. She is thinking about taking a buyout package from her job and running her aromatherapy business, which she launched on the side two years ago, full time. Most of the start-up funds came from her savings. She experienced immediate success. She might break even this year and make a profit in the next two years. The buyout package would give her a year's salary, or about $60,000 after taxes. She would need to invest half of that money in the business and live off the other half. Rhonda could also borrow from her 401(k), which has almost $200,000 in it. She can't afford to pay herself a salary right away and would have to depend on the severance money. She knows that she could be jeopardizing her retirement savings. She isn't sure whether she should invest part of the money that she would receive or leverage those funds to have more money to invest in the business. If you were Rhonda, what would you do?

Mrs. Roberts is a 70-year-old widow. In the nine months since her husband died, she hasn't done anything with the insurance money she received. More than $100,000 has been sitting in a money market account earning 5 percent. She doesn't need the money to live on right now, provided that she keeps her expenses low. All she has to pay are the mortgage and utilities. She will continue to receive her husband's pension check, but it is now reduced by half. She has money in IRAs that totals another $50,000. If she plays her cards right, she can manage. She's wavering between paying off the mortgage and investing the insurance money. She doesn't have any real investing experience and doesn't know where to begin. If you were Mrs. Roberts, what would you do?

Chapter 18

Putting Your Portfolio Together

The Bottom Line

Creating your own portfolio, alone or with your partner, is a very empowering act. It fuels a sense of ownership over your life and opens a wide world of new information and interests.

Like an artist who carefully chooses which paintings to place in her artist's portfolio, you need to carefully select which investment products to place in your investment portfolio.

The Three Questions

Your portfolio choices will be a result of the answers you give to the three questions I posed in previous chapters:

1. What do I want the money to do? (your goal or objective)
2. When will I need the money? (your time frame)
3. How much risk can I afford to take? (your risk tolerance)

Your answers to these questions will direct you to the appropriate investment products. The products will produce one of the following:

1. Income (Choose this if you want income now.)
2. Growth (Choose this if you want your money to grow over time.)
3. Growth and income (Choose this if you want your money to both grow and produce immediate income.)

Once you determine whether you want income, growth, or both, you'll know what category of investment products to pursue. For example, consider these scenarios:

1. If you want income, you'll shop for bonds.
2. If you want growth, you'll shop for stocks.
3. If you want growth and income, you'll shop for stocks and bonds.

Now let me ask you two other questions to help you narrow your choices further:

1. How much money do you have to invest this month?
2. How much time do you want to spend on the actual process of investing?

With regard to the first question, we've already determined that in today's investment market, you can invest as little as $25 per month or as much as you want. If you're currently limited to the $25 per month alternative, you will be choosing from a relatively small number of mutual funds. If you want to choose from a full range of mutual funds, you can begin depositing money into a money market fund until you've saved enough to purchase the mutual fund of your choice.

Your answer to the question of how much time you want to spend on the actual process of investing will cue you to whether you want to take a hands-on or hands-off approach. If you want hands-on, you will want to do your own research and maybe even your own trading of stocks or mutual funds. If you want hands-off, you will let someone else manage your investments. Of course, you can have a bit of both. This is your portfolio, and you are in charge of it.

Charlene

Let's imagine that Charlene and you and I are in the same room, and that it is Charlene's turn to answer the questions I've posed. Let's listen to her answers and see how they work together to determine her portfolio.

Summary of Charlene's Situation

1. Charlene has a student loan obligation that she has to repay.
2. She is interested in buying a new car.
3. Her employers offer a retirement plan into which they will contribute 50 percent on her behalf, up to 6 percent of her salary.

Charlene's Answers to the Big Three Questions

1. *What do I want the money to do?* "I'm not sure. I've just completed a tremendous goal by earning my college degree. Now I'd just like to live a little: buy a new car and pay off college loans. Still, I hear that if I start investing now, when I'm this young, it will be much easier to reach my goals in retirement, whatever they are."
2. *When will I need the money?* "I'm making pretty good money, so I don't really need my investments to pay off now. I'll need them later, in about 25 years."
3. *How much risk can I afford to take?* "I'm not concerned. I'm young."

Coaching Tip

You are absolutely unique. Nobody is exactly like you, so your financial plan won't be exactly like anybody else's. The more you know yourself, the more likely your financial plan will meet your needs.

Charlene's Choices

Charlene's answers take her one step closer to selecting her portfolio.

What Charlene wants: She wants her money to grow long-term. Conclusion: She's after growth.

When she will need the money: She figures that she will need the money in about 25 years. Conclusion: She will leave it in for the long haul.

Risk: Because she will leave it in for the long haul, and because time is on her side, Charlene can bear higher risk.

How much money she needs to invest now: $50 per month.

Hands-on or hands-off: Because Charlene has so much time to invest and is still deciding what her retirement goals are and what she wants her money to do for her, her approach will be hands-off.

Charlene's Investment Portfolio

Based on her answers, Charlene's portfolio will begin quite simply, with her employer's retirement plan, through an automatic deduction of her paycheck. However, she has a critical decision to make about the new car she wants to buy. Will it cramp her budget too much to buy new?

My Comments

Charlene has done well in graduating from college. Not surprisingly, she seems to lack a clear set of long-term financial goals, which is common among young people just completing college. She does acknowledge that she wants to have enough money in her retirement years to maintain the lifestyle that she plans to enjoy before retirement. Yet she also wants a new car.

In the meantime, she has student loans to pay off and some decisions to make about how to use the income she's earning now.

Let's look at the decision to buy this new car. Charlene can visit www. cars.com to determine exactly how much the car of her dream will cost. She will find that after financing, it will be almost $29,000 dollars. She will also be able to determine the amount of her monthly payments. The calculator on this site will determine that her payment on a five-year car loan of that amount will be around $465 per month. The site www.insweb.com can determine exactly how much her insurance cost will be. Her insurance will cost another $100 a month. All totaled, this decision could end up costing her almost $600 a month.

An alternative would be to purchase a car that is a few years older and that costs a lot less. A Volkswagen Jetta that is two years old would bring her payments down to less than $300. The additional funds could then be used to start making contributions to her employer plan. Starting that plan right now with her employer match rather than waiting 5 or 10 years to get started adds up to some serious dollars, as you can see from the accompanying chart.

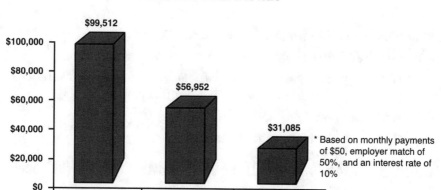

The Cost of Waiting
Charlene's Retirement Portfolio in 25 Years*

* Based on monthly payments of $50, employer match of 50%, and an interest rate of 10%

It is also imperative for Charlene to begin investing now because women leave the workforce more often to care for families. She will need an early and strong start to compensate for what she will lose financially. She is in a good place to set herself up for life.

So, Charlene should invest for her retirement using a growth fund through her employer. Hopefully, she will add other growth products to her portfolio using the money that she saves buying the Jetta instead of the Passat. She should pay off her student loans through an automatic payroll deduction plan.

Rhonda

Now let's turn our attention to Rhonda. Rhonda is also faced with some tremendous financial decisions. Rhonda is leaving the safety and security of a lifetime corporate career to embark on a business venture fraught with risk and unknown outcomes. Rhonda is also at a critical stage of life. She is in her early 40s, when most people earn their highest wages. Is starting a business and jeopardizing her accomplishments a good decision?

Let's review and prioritize Rhonda's issues:

1. She's about to lose her income.
2. She will receive a lump sum of $60,000 in severance.
3. She needs capital to fund her business.
4. She will no longer be contributing to a retirement plan through an employer, but she does have almost $200,000 from her 401(k) account.

5. She is now responsible for her own health and disability insurance.

Rhonda's Answers to the Big Three Questions About Her Severance Money

1. *What do I want the severance money to do?* "I want the severance money to provide income while I build my business."
2. *When will I need the money?* "Immediately."
3. *How much risk can I afford to take?* "None."

Rhonda's Answers to The Big Three Questions About Her 401(k) Money

1. *What do I want the 401(k) money to do?* "I want it to fund my retirement."
2. *When will I need the money?* "I have more than 20 years before I'm 65. But I may retire earlier, if I can afford to."
3. *How much risk can I afford to take?* "I have to invest for growth and can still invest rather aggressively, provided that I don't have to take a loan from it for my business."

Rhonda's Choices

Rhonda's answers take her one step closer to selecting her portfolio.

What Rhonda wants: She wants income from the $60,000 severance and retirement from her 401(k).

When she will need the money: She'll need money immediately (from the severance) and at retirement (from the 401[k]). So, her time frame is both near-future and long term.

Risk: Because she needs to invest for growth, she can bear a moderate amount of risk with her 401(k), but none with her severance.

How much money to invest now: Almost $200,000 in 401(k); $60,000 in severance pay.

Hands-on or hands-off: Both, because the 401(k) has time to grow and because the severance will fund her business.

Rhonda's Investment Portfolio

Based on her answers, Rhonda's portfolio should include a money market account with check-writing for liquidity (she may want it in a money market mutual fund because of the large amount) and mutual funds for growth and retirement.

My Comments

Let's look at Rhonda's first issue: the severance money. The $60,000 represents 12 months of her income. Ideally, she should have at least six months ($30,000) in a fairly liquid and accessible account. However, because she is self-employed, she needs to keep the full amount in a liquid account. This is especially true because she doesn't think that she will be able to pay herself a salary for a period of time.

Now let's look at the money in her 401(k) accounts. Rhonda had great success with her retirement investment and should look at preserving this money at all costs. Taking a loan for her business from these funds would result in penalties and taxes to the tune of almost 40 percent. She would be better off taking out a small business loan. Take a look at the following chart to see how much her existing balance could appreciate if she leaves it alone. Rhonda can understand how these decisions will affect her by visiting www.investor.nasd.com and using the site's calculators to determine how much her savings will grow.

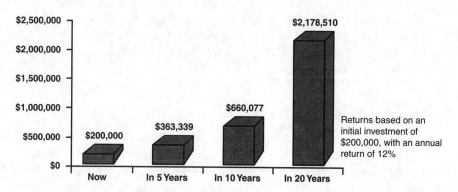

What Would Happen to Rhonda's $200,000 if She Left It Alone?

- Now: $200,000
- In 5 Years: $363,339
- In 10 Years: $660,077
- In 20 Years: $2,178,510

Returns based on an initial investment of $200,000, with an annual return of 12%

If she withdraws $50,000 and pays taxes and penalties, it would result in a net amount of less than $30,000. In addition, look at the following chart to see the impact that investing $50,000 less would have on Rhonda's retirement savings.

In 20 years, the cost to Rhonda's future would equal a loss of earnings (from $200,000) of almost $400,000. That's why she should look into the small business loan.

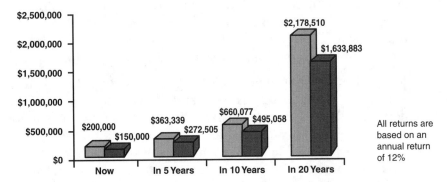

Rhonda Stands to Lose a Lot More Than $50,000 if She Dips into Her Retirement Funds

All returns are based on an annual return of 12%

Rhonda is taking a big risk by taking the retirement package. However, she is following her dream.

Women are starting businesses at a rate that is twice that of men. Rhonda needs to make a huge investment of research and planning to ensure the success of her business. Going from part-time distributor to full-time business owner, where she depends on the business for income, is a leap. Rhonda should continue to look for ways to fund her business without jeopardizing her personal assets. The Small Business Administration has a Web site (www.sba.gov) that can assist her in developing a solid business plan and alternative financing.

Mrs. Roberts

Mrs. Roberts poses the greatest challenge of all. She is now a widow and is trying to navigate her way through a financial maze without the benefit of experience. She is almost 70 years old and cannot afford to risk or lose her principal. Her husband had handled the finances, and she doesn't want to make any mistakes. This feeling of uncertainty has left her paralyzed. Based on what you've learned so far, what should she do?

Let's review and prioritize Mrs. Roberts' issues:

1. She is on a fixed income.
2. Her pension income has been reduced by half.

3. She has a lump sum of money that needs to be invested.

4. She has no investment experience or knowledge.

Mrs. Roberts' Answers to the Big Three Questions

1. *What do I want my money to do?* "I want the money to provide income."

2. *When will I need the money?* "Immediately."

3. *How much risk can I afford to take?* "Very little."

Mrs. Roberts' Choices

Mrs. Roberts' answers will take her one step closer to selecting her portfolio.

What Mrs. Roberts wants: She wants income.

When she will need the money: Immediately. Her time frame is short-term.

Risk: Because she is on a fixed income late in life, Mrs. Roberts' risk tolerance is low.

How much money to invest now: More than $100,000.

Hands-on or hands-off: Because she has no investment experience or knowledge, she will need an adviser. Hands-off.

Mrs. Roberts' Portfolio

Mrs. Roberts wants income at low risk, so her investment product should be bonds. She should add this to the other investment products that she and her husband had selected before his death.

My Comments

Mrs. Roberts now realizes that the best use of this money will probably be to create additional income. If she wants to get an idea of how much income she could expect to receive, she can look in the business section of the newspaper. The current rates on treasuries, certificates of deposit, and loans are usually listed there. The highest amount that she can earn in this current environment is around 6 percent. If she invests the $100,000, she could expect to receive approximately $6,000 a year, or $500 a month in interest. The yield or return on treasuries can be used as a benchmark from which she can evaluate other strategies. If someone offers her a higher return, she will know that she is taking on more risk.

At the suggestion of her children, Mrs. Roberts made an appointment with the financial adviser who handled her husband's account. Here is what he recommended:

Description	Average Maturity	Current Yield	Amount of Investment	Approx. Annual Income
U.S. Treasury Bond 6's "10	6 years	6.00	$25,000	1,500.00
Strong Advantage Mutual Fund	3.5 Years	5.47	$25,000	1,367.50
Fidelity Short Term Bond Fund	3	6.66	$25,000	1,665.00
Asset Management Money Market	90 days	4.9625	$25,000	1,240.60
Total			$100,000	5,772.60

The adviser suggested that Mrs. Roberts invest the money in different types of bonds and bond funds. He used a laddering strategy by investing most of it in short-term bond mutual funds and buying treasuries to lock in the 6 percent yield for 10 years. The income from the bond funds will fluctuate, but if she needs money or decides to change strategies, she can always liquidate them and reinvest in another type of investment.

The adviser also left $25,000 in a liquid money market account until Mrs. Roberts decided whether she wanted to pay down her mortgage. After reviewing his suggestion with her children, she decided to invest rather than pay down the mortgage. The income wasn't great, but at least she felt that the money was safe. She left the money that was invested in IRAs in stock mutual funds because she trusted her husband's judgment and because she had watched it grow over the years. She felt comfortable with her decision for now. What would you have done? Do you think that the adviser was on target?

Different Needs, Same Process

As you can see, Charlene, Rhonda, and Mrs. Roberts all had different needs. However, the process that we used to evaluate their situations and identify a strategy was the same. What do you want your money to do? How long do you have? How much risk can you afford to take? This is the investment selection process that you can use as you continue your financial journey. You can choose to do it alone or to use an adviser. It's the process that is most important.

It's Your Turn

There you have it, the path to confident investing. Wherever you are on that path, millions of other women and I are there with you. We're doing it!

The Bottom Line

Your portfolio is your expression of belief in your financial future and your ability to make good choices for it.

Reader's Journal:

Knowledge Gained:

_____
_____
_____
_____
_____
_____
_____
_____
_____

Steps I Will Take:

_____
_____
_____
_____
_____
_____
_____
_____
_____

Appendix A

Worksheets

Net Worth

Date: _____

	Total	Self	Spouse	Joint
Assets (What You Own)				
Cash or Equivalents				
Cash	_____	_____	_____	_____
Checking accounts	_____	_____	_____	_____
Savings accounts	_____	_____	_____	_____
Money market fund	_____	_____	_____	_____
Certificates of deposit (CDs)	_____	_____	_____	_____
Savings bonds/treasuries	_____	_____	_____	_____
Life insurance (cash value)	_____	_____	_____	_____
Total	_____	_____	_____	_____
Invested Assets				
Retirement Assets				
IRA accounts	_____	_____	_____	_____
Pension/profit sharing	_____	_____	_____	_____
401(k), 403(b), 457 plans	_____	_____	_____	_____
Keogh accounts	_____	_____	_____	_____
Annuities (surrender value)	_____	_____	_____	_____
Other	_____	_____	_____	_____
Investments				
Stocks	_____	_____	_____	_____
Bonds	_____	_____	_____	_____
Mutual funds	_____	_____	_____	_____
Government securities	_____	_____	_____	_____
Rental property	_____	_____	_____	_____
Business equity	_____	_____	_____	_____
Receivables (money owed you)	_____	_____	_____	_____
Limited partnerships	_____	_____	_____	_____

Invested Assets

Retirement Assets

Patents, copyrights

Trusts

Other

Total

Personal Property

Home

Vacation home

Automobiles

Household furnishings

Clothes and jewelry

Antiques, collectibles

Boats, RVs, etc.

Other

Total

Total Assets $_____ $_____ $_____ $_____

Liabilities (What You Owe)

Debts

Medical/dental

Taxes owed

Education loans

Alimony

Child support

Mortgage

Business loans

Personal loans

Pledges

Contracts

Property taxes owed

Mortgage on rental property

(continued)

Liabilities (What You Owe)

Debts
Home-equity loans

Credit card debt

Other

Total Liabilities $_____ $_____ $_____ $_____

Total Assets $_____ $_____ $_____ $_____

Minus Total Liabilities $_____ $_____ $_____ $_____

Net Worth $_____ $_____ $_____ $_____

Copyright © 1993, Harvard Financial Educators (Reprinted with permission.)

Cash Flow

Income

	Monthly	Annual
Salary		
Salary/spouse		
Self-employment income		
Social Security		
Social Security (spouse)		
Pension		
Pension (spouse)		
Rental income		
Interest		
Dividends		
Capital gains		
Alimony received		
Child support		
Other		
Other		

Budget Worksheet

Basic Expenses

Item	Weekly	Monthly	Yearly
Home Expenses			
Mortgage/rent			
Real estate taxes			
Special assessment			
Home-equity loan			

Basic Expenses (continued)

Item	Weekly	Monthly	Yearly
Second Home Expenses			
Mortgage	_____	_____	_____
Real estate taxes	_____	_____	_____
Other Expenses	_____	_____	_____
Apartment			
Rent	_____	_____	_____
Parking fees	_____	_____	_____
Other fees	_____	_____	_____
Grounds Maintenance			
Lawn service	_____	_____	_____
Rubbish removal	_____	_____	_____
Snow removal	_____	_____	_____
Supplies and equipment	_____	_____	_____
Tree and shrub care	_____	_____	_____
Other	_____	_____	_____
Utilities			
Electric	_____	_____	_____
Water	_____	_____	_____
Oil	_____	_____	_____
Telephone	_____	_____	_____
Gas	_____	_____	_____
Insurance			
Homeowners	_____	_____	_____
Umbrella	_____	_____	_____
Household			
Groceries	_____	_____	_____
Cleaning supplies, etc.	_____	_____	_____
Clothing			
Family	_____	_____	_____
Dry cleaning	_____	_____	_____

Item	Weekly	Monthly	Yearly
Healthcare			
Insurance			
Doctor			
Prescriptions/medications			
Dentist			
Other			
Auto Expenses			
Loan payment			
Gasoline			
Repairs and maintenance			
Insurance			
Registration, license, inspection			
Tolls			
Parking			
Other			
Transportation			
Bus, train, subway			
Life Insurance Premiums			
Policy 1			
Policy 2			
Disability Insurance Premiums			
Policy 1			
Alimony and Child Support			
Alimony			
Child support			
Work-Related			
Union dues			
Continuing education			
Other			

(continued)

Item	Weekly	Monthly	Yearly
Childcare			
Daycare	_____	_____	_____
Miscellaneous			
Bank charge	_____	_____	_____
Postage	_____	_____	_____
Financial—tax prep, legal	_____	_____	_____
Other	_____	_____	_____

Appendix B

Glossary

10-K *See* **annual report.**

10-Q *See* **quarterly report.**

12(b)1 fees Fees assessed to some mutual fund shareholders for marketing expense of the investment company; trail commission charged by some mutual fund companies typically on B shares and C shares. *See also* **commission.**

13-Week Treasury Bill-IRX The T-bill index that is based on the most recently auctioned 13-week T-bill. *See also* **Treasury bill (T-bill).**

401(k) A tax-qualified retirement plan for employees of for-profit companies. Employees can contribute a percentage of earned income by payroll deduction. The employer can contribute to the employee's account or match employee contributions, based on a percentage of earnings. *See also* **qualified retirement plan.**

403(b) A tax-qualified retirement plan for employees of non-profit companies, such as schools, churches, and municipalities. Employees can contribute a percentage of earned income by payroll deduction. The employer can contribute to the employee's account or match employee contributions, based on a percentage of earnings. *See also* **qualified retirement plan.**

accrued interest Interest that is earned or due since the last interest payment date, but that hasn't yet been paid to the bondholder. This becomes an issue when bonds change hands between interest payment dates. The purchase price of the bond will equal the market value of the bond plus the accrued interest due. The accrued interest paid at time of purchase is returned to the new bondholder when the next scheduled interest payment is made.

accumulation phase The period during which assets are invested and accumulating tax-deferred growth and income within an annuity contract. The period in an annuity's life before distributions to the annuitant begin.

adjusted basis An investor's net amount at risk in an investment; this would include the original investment plus all reinvested dividends or capital gains, minus prior withdrawals. Net sales proceeds minus adjusted basis equals taxable gain.

adjusted gross income (AGI) Taken from the individual's income tax return, this term means total annual income, minus tax-exempt income, minus other adjustments to income such as deductible IRA contributions and self-employed health insurance premiums.

ADRs *See* **American Depository Receipts.**

AGI *See* **adjusted gross income.**

American Depository Receipts (ADRs) A foreign security that is repackaged as an American security so that American investors can own the securities valued in U.S. dollars. A U.S. bank creates ADRs based on evidence of ownership of a specified number of shares of a foreign security, with the underlying shares held in a depository in the foreign company. A negotiable certificate representing ownership of the foreign securities is traded in the American securities markets.

American Stock Exchange (AMEX)   A private, not-for-profit organization located in New York City that handles roughly one fifth of all securities transactions in the United States.

annual report   A company's annual report to shareholders. This report includes information about finances, management, and operations. All publicly traded companies must submit this report to the SEC annually. This annual SEC filing is known as the 10-K report.

annuitant   The person who is entitled to receive the distributions from an annuity contract.

annuities   A contract between an insurance company and an individual; annuities provide tax-deferred growth and income to the investor. Generally, in return for either a lump-sum payment or a series of payments, the company will guarantee an income stream, typically for the annuitant's lifetime or some other specified period. *See also* **fixed annuity, annuitant, accumulation phase, annuitize, payout phase**, and **separate account.**

annuitize   To settle with an insurance company in exchange for a stream of payments from an annuity contract.

arbitrage   A simultaneous purchase of a security in one market and the sale of the same or a similar security in another market in an attempt to profit from the price difference between the two markets.

arbitration   A process of conflict resolution that involves a knowledgeable third party.

arbitrator   A private, disinterested person involved in a process to help conflicting parties resolve their disputes.

asset   Any possession that has value upon exchange.

asset allocation   A rational process of diversification of an investor's assets among different asset classes, taking into account all characteristics of the investor's financial situation and investment objectives.

asset management company   A company that manages money on behalf of clients; clients pay management fees usually based upon total assets under management.

average annual return (AAR)   A measure of total investment performance, including growth plus dividend yield, shown as an average total return per year, over a stated period of time. *See also* **return on investment.**

balance sheet A financial statement that provides a snapshot of a person's or business's financial position. A listing of assets, net worth, and liabilities as of a specific date. *See also* **financial statement.**

"blue chip" stocks A term used to describe well-established companies that are known for sound management along with an excellent track record of consistent profits and dividend payments. The term is derived from the blue poker chip, which has the greatest exchange value.

bond A fixed-income security that is a legal obligation of the issuing company or government to repay the loan principal to bondholders on a specified date. In addition, the issuer promises to pay interest to the bondholder at a rate stated on the face of the bond certificate.

bond laddering *See* **laddering.**

bondholder The owner of a fixed-income security.

"book entry only" A security that is sold without delivery of the actual certificate. Records of ownership are maintained in a central location.

Boston Stock Exchange The third oldest stock exchange in the United States, and the first stock exchange to offer memberships to foreign broker/dealers.

callable bond A bond that is issued with a provision that allows the issuer to redeem the bond before its stated maturity date.

capital appreciation Increase in value as a result of growth. An increase in the market price of a stock.

capital gain Taxable income that represents the increase in value of a security in comparison to its adjusted basis. *See also* **adjusted basis.**

capital gains distributions Required payments made to mutual fund shareholders on capital gains that were realized by the fund on the sale of fund portfolio securities. These distributions are usually made in late December and are included in the shareholder's taxable income. Capital gains distributions increase the adjusted basis of the shareholder.

capital losses Taxable income that represents the increase in value of a security in comparison to its adjusted basis. *See also* **adjusted basis.**

capitalization *See* **market capitalization** and **capitalize.**

capitalize As used in reference to debt, a method of combining several loans into a single loan with an extended repayment term of up to 30 years. This can be an effective method of lowering your monthly payment. As used in reference to investing, to use or convert to capital, to establish the stock of a new business at a certain price, or to supply capital to a business.

cash flow analysis   A financial analysis of cash inflows and outflows for a stated period of time, taking into account all sources of income and expenses.

cash flow statement   A financial statement that provides detailed information about income and expenses over a specific period of time. *See also* **financial statement.**

CDSC   *See* **contingent deferred sales charge.**

certified financial planner (CFP)   An individual trained in all areas of financial planning who has passed a rigorous national certifying exam, abides by a professional code of ethics, and meets the continuing educational requirements of the professional organization.

certified public accountant (CPA)   An individual trained in accounting and taxation who has passed a rigorous national certifying exam, abides by a professional code of ethics, and meets the continuing educational requirements of the professional organization.

CFP   *See* **certified financial planner.**

checkbook investing   An approach to investing that is based on buying those companies that produce products that an investor routinely buys as a consumer.

churning   Excessive trading in a customer's account by the broker or registered representative, a violation of the NASD Rules of Fair Practice.

cliff vesting   A schedule of vesting that allows no vesting of benefits for a number of years, followed by 100 percent vesting.

commercial paper   An unsecured short-term promissory note issued by corporations to raise capital for short-term needs such as inventory or financing accounts receivable.

commission   Income received as a result of marketing a product or service, usually stated as a percentage of the sale price of the product. Registered representatives, brokers, and insurance representatives are typically compensated by commissions.

common stock   A security that represents ownership in a corporation. Holders of common stock have the right to vote for corporate directors and policy. They share in the unlimited growth potential of the company, as well as in any losses experienced by the company, but only to the extent of stock ownership. Common stockholders are entitled to receive dividends after preferred stockholders have been paid. In the event of bankruptcy, common stockholders stand last in line, after all creditors, bondholders, and preferred stockholders are paid in full. The most that a common stockholder stands to lose is the full investment.

compound interest   Interest that is paid or received on interest from prior periods. *See also* **simple interest.**

confidence   A belief in one's own ability; a firm belief or trust; certainty of personal assurance.

Consumer Price Index (CPI) The U.S. Bureau of Labor publishes this measure monthly. It is the primary indicator of inflation in the U.S. economy and takes into account price changes on consumer goods, including food, housing, and transportation.

contingent deferred sales charge (CDSC)   *See also* **surrender charge.** Typically, this is a reducing charge over a limited period of years. A charge imposed by the insurance company upon termination or surrender of a life insurance contract or annuity. A sales charge imposed upon the surrender of B or C shares of mutual funds.

contrarian   A person who thinks and acts contrary to conventional wisdom when it comes to investing. If the majority of investors are bullish, the contrarian is bearish, and vice versa.

convertible security   A fixed-income security such as a bond or preferred stock that can be converted to common stock at the owner's discretion. Because bondholders have the rights to income and the potential to participate in the growth of the company, the issuer can pay a slightly lower rate of interest on these bonds and still attract investors.

coupon bonds   Older form of bond or debt obligation with interest payment coupons attached to the actual bond certificate. Coupons need to be "clipped" every 6 months and submitted to the trustee in exchange for semiannual interest payments—hence the term "coupon clipper" for someone who lives on bond interest income.

coupon rate   The interest rate stated on the face of a bond as a percentage of face value or par value. *See also* **nominal yield.**

coupons   *See* **coupon bonds.**

covered option   Options that are sold by an investor who owns the underlying security.

CPA *See* **certified public accountant.**

CPI *See* **Consumer Price Index.**

credit rating A measure of a company's credit-worthiness as determined by an independent rating company such as Moody's or Standard & Poor. The better the credit rating, the more credit-worthy the underlying company.

current assets Readily accessible assets that are held as cash or that can be easily converted to cash. Liquid assets such as cash, or money held in a checking or savings account or money market fund or account.

current liabilities Debts that are due within a short period of time, typically one to six months.

current price *See* **public offering price.**

current yield The annual return on a security, determined by dividing the total interest or dividends paid by the security's market price.

CUSIP An identifying number assigned to every security by the Committee on Uniform Securities Identification Procedures.

custodial account An account set up and managed for the benefit of a minor or a retirement account shareholder.

custodian The organization responsible for the management and safekeeping of a custodial account; an institution responsible for the management and administration of a mutual fund or retirement account.

day order An order to buy or sell a security that is valid only until the close of trading on the day the order is entered.

day trader An investor in securities or commodities who opens and closes positions within a day.

debenture An unsecured promissory note issued by a corporation.

default risk The risk that a bond issue will default on interest payments or on the repayment of principal to the investor.

deficit spending Spending that exceeds income over a given period of time.

defined benefit plan A qualified retirement plan that is designed to provide a specified benefit to all participants upon retirement.

derivative An investment product whose value is based on the value of an underlying security.

direct investment plans Companies that provide for the direct purchase of stock from the issuing company.

discount broker A broker who charges lower commission rates for buying and selling securities than a full-service broker. These brokers typically provide order execution services only and provide no advice or research for the investor.

discount rate The interest rate that the Federal Reserve charges banks for overnight loans.

diversification The investment practice of not keeping all your eggs in one basket. Diversification across asset classes and within asset classes reduces unsystematic risk and portfolio volatility.

dividend A share of after-tax company earnings that is paid to shareholders of record. Most dividends are paid in cash but are sometimes paid in additional shares of stock of the same or a different company. Dividends are declared quarterly by the company board of directors.

dividend reinvestment The purchase of additional shares of the same company with dividends from currently owned shares.

dividend reinvestment plans Plans that automatically reinvest shareholders' dividends into more shares of stock instead of cash.

dollar cost averaging A system of buying mutual fund shares in fixed intervals of time for a fixed dollar amount, regardless of the price of the shares. The average cost per share is reduced over time as the investor buys more shares of the fund when the price is low, and fewer shares when the price is high.

Dow Jones Industrial Average (DJIA) The "Dow," the most widely used market indicator composed of 30 large, actively traded industrial companies.

DRIPS *See* **dividend reinvestment plans.**

earnings per share Total company earnings (income minus expenses, after taxes) for a stated period of time, divided by the number of outstanding shares of stock, including capital stock.

education IRA An IRA for use in educational planning. A maximum contribution of $500 per year per student under age 18 can be made. Contributions are not income tax–deductible, but earnings accumulate on a tax-deferred basis and are tax-free if used for education, including tuition, books, or room and board. There are income limitations for tax-free withdrawals.

EE bonds Nonmarketable U.S. government securities, meaning that they cannot be used as collateral and are nonnegotiable and nontransferable. They can be purchased from the Treasury Department through various issuing agencies, including commercial banks and post offices. These bonds are issued as discount bonds at 50 percent of face value in denominations of $50 to $10,000. They accrue interest over the life of the bond and even beyond the maturity date. These bonds can be redeemed prior to maturity, at maturity, and after maturity, but only by the purchaser or beneficiary. Interest earned is state and municipal tax–exempt. Tax on accrued interest can be paid annually or deferred until maturity or redemption. *See also* **U.S. savings bonds.**

EFC Expected family contribution, per the federal formula for determining federal financial aid. *See also* **expected family contribution** and **Free Application for Federal Student Aid.**

Employee Retirement Security Act of 1974 The federal law that governs the operation of corporate pension and benefit plans.

EPS *See* **earnings per share.**

ERISA *See* **Employee Retirement Security Act of 1974.**

ex-date The first date on which a security would trade without the buyer being entitled to receive declared dividends.

ex-dividend date *See* **ex-date.**

expected family contribution The amount that the federal government has determined that a student and family should be able to contribute toward the cost of education, including living expenses, for one year. The expected family contribution is calculated by a standard formula, applied to all financial aid applicants nationally, that takes into consideration all the information included on the Free Application for Federal Student Aid (FAFSA). The expected family contribution is the same for all schools, without regard to the cost of the school. *See also* **Free Application for Federal Financial Aid.**

expiration date The date upon which an option expires.

face value The amount noted on the face of a bond certificate.

FAFSA *See* **Free Application for Federal Student Aid.**

fee-based planner A financial planner who is compensated by fees paid for services rendered. Fees can be charged on an hourly basis, or a flat fee can be charged for services. In addition, fees can be charged for asset management and commission income received for product sales and support.

fee-only planner A financial planner who is compensated only by fees paid for services rendered.

financial statement A statement of financial values that represents cash flow or net worth of an individual or company.

fixed annuity An annuity contract that guarantees both interest and principal. Upon distribution, regular annuity payments are guaranteed for lifetime or another period of time.

fixed-income security A debt security that is designed to provide regular, fixed income to the investor.

Free Application for Federal Student Aid (FAFSA) The mandatory application required for a student to receive consideration for virtually all forms of financial aid. To determine a student's level of financial need, the U.S. Department of Education uses a standard formula, established by Congress, to evaluate the information included on the Free Application for Federal Student Aid. On the basis of this formula, the expected family contribution (EFC) and student contribution levels are established. *See also* **EFC.**

full-service broker A broker who trades all securities in addition to providing research and investment advice.

"going public" *See* **initial public offering** and **public offering.**

good until canceled order A market order that stands until filled or canceled.

HELOC *See* **home equity line of credit.**

HH bonds Nonmarketable U.S. government securities, meaning that they cannot be used as collateral and are nonnegotiable and nontransferable. They are purchased from the Treasury Department in denominations of $500 to $10,000 through various issuing agencies, including commercial banks and post offices. These bonds pay interest income semiannually, mature in 10 years, and can be redeemed at any time only by the purchaser or beneficiary. Interest earned is state and municipal tax–exempt.

home equity line of credit A flexible line of credit against the accumulated equity of a residence, typically a second mortgage, with a variable interest rate charged on the outstanding credit balance only. Interest is generally charged on the average daily balance. Minimum payment due is sometimes interest only, or interest plus 1 to 2 percent of the outstanding balance. Payments in excess of the required minimum can (and should) be made at any time without prepayment penalty.

home equity loan   A fixed loan against the accumulated equity of a residence, typically a second mortgage, usually for a fixed period of time (typically 1 to 10 years) at a fixed rate of interest with a fixed monthly payment. HE loans can also be variable-rate loans. *See also* **home equity line of credit.**

inflation risk   The risk that purchasing power will decline as a result of inflation.

initial public offering   An offering of stock to the public by a company for the first time. Also commonly known as an IPO.

interest   Usually stated as a percentage or dollar amount. For debt, money you must pay for the privilege of borrowing money, expressed as a percentage of the outstanding principal. For fixed-income investments, the yield or return on an investment. This is income received as a result of lending money.

inverted yield curve   A chart that compares interest paid on debt securities over different periods of time. The normal yield curve represents higher bond yields as bond maturities increase. The inverted yield curve shows lower bond yields as bond maturities increase.

investment assets   Assets that are held by an individual or business with an expectation of return of income or growth of principal. Not a personal use asset; these are portfolio assets.

investment banker   A firm, acting as underwriter or agent, that serves as intermediary between an issuer of securities and the investing public.

investment objective   An investor's stated financial goals.

investor   A person who buys or sells securities for his own account or the accounts of others.

issuer   The company that is distributing securities that have been registered with the SEC to the public.

laddering   An approach to buying bonds or other fixed-income securities that have a staggered series of maturity dates. The rationale is that with staggered maturities, the investor has broader diversification within the fixed-securities market, a higher yield as a result of buying longer-term instruments, and a measure of liquidity as a result of knowing that a security will be maturing on a regular schedule.

large-cap companies Companies that have a market capitalization of $5 billion or more. Market capitalization is the number of outstanding shares multiplied by the share price.

liability An obligation to pay; a responsibility.

liquid assets Cash or other assets that can easily be converted into cash. *See* **current assets.**

long-term capital gain Taxable gain on the sale of a security that has been held for more than one year.

margin A purchase of securities using credit that has been extended by a broker/dealer. Margin trading is speculative and heavily regulated by the NASD and the Federal Reserve Board. *See also* **Regulation T.**

margin call If the equity in portfolio is less than the maintenance margin requirement, the account is said to be under-margined. A margin call is issued.

market capitalization The price of a stock multiplied by the total number of outstanding shares. Also, a publicly traded company's total valuation.

market order An order to buy or sell a security at the best available price when the order is received in the market.

market risk The potential for loss of value of a stock as a result of normal fluctuations in the market. Also known as systematic risk because it is risk that is shared across the entire market system and is not specific to one stock or sector.

market timing An attempt to manage investments in a way that tries to anticipate changes in the market or market sectors.

maturity date The date on which a financial contract becomes due, as in the case of a loan, CD, or bond instrument.

money manager An individual or business institution that makes investment management decisions for investors for a fee.

Morningstar Reports A well-recognized company involved with the rating of securities.

naked option An option that is bought or sold without the ownership of the underlying security.

NASDAQ The NASDAQ Stock Market, established in 1971, is the first fully electronic stock market.

NASDAQ Small-Cap Market A market made up of more than 1,400 small-cap companies that want to be available on an exchange, that have applied for the listing, and that meet specific financial requirements.

NASDAQ-100 An index of the largest 100 nonfinancial stocks on NASDAQ, weighted according to their capitalization.

National Association of Investors Corporation (NAIC) A nonprofit organization involved with helping to establish investment clubs.

National Association of Securities Dealers (NASD) A self-regulatory organization (SRO) that oversees the activities of the over-the-counter market, established by the 1938 Maloney Act.

National Association of Securities Dealers Automated Quotations, (NASDAQ) The organization that is responsible for administering the NASDAQ stock market.

NAV *See* **net asset value.**

negative cash flow When expenses exceed income for the given period. *See also* **deficit spending.**

net asset value The market value of a mutual fund share; its bid price. The NAV is calculated at the close of the exchange each business day and is determined by taking the combined values of all securities owned, plus other fund assets such as cash, minus any fund liabilities outstanding, and then dividing the result by the total number of outstanding fund shares.

net worth statement A measure of value. Total assets minus total liabilities equals net worth.

nominal yield The interest rate stated on the face of a bond. *See also* **coupon rate.**

over-the-counter markets (OTC) Where unlisted stocks trade.

P/E ratio *See* **price-to-earnings ratio.**

payout phase The phase at which an annuitant decides how to withdraw from an annuity.

Pell Grant A needs-based grant for undergraduate students. It is the first level of funding of the financial aid package; other federal and private aid is added to it. Because the Pell Grant is a grant, it does not need to be paid back. The maximum award for the 1999–2000 award year was $3,125. The Pell Grant is awarded to all eligible students, but the amounts for future awards will depend on program funding.

pension plan Typically a defined-benefit retirement plan. *See also* **qualified retirement plan.**

Perkins Loan A low-interest (5 percent) loan available to both undergraduate and graduate students who have exceptional financial need. This need is determined by a federal formula using the information provided on the

Free Application for Federal Student Aid (FAFSA). The loan is made with government funds, but the school is the lender.

personal financial adviser (PFA) A financial planner who has at least five years of professional experience and has passed a series of exams. This is a fairly new designation that was created by the National Association of Securities Dealers.

personal use assets Assets owned by an individual for personal use or enjoyment.

placing a trade An execution of an order to buy or sell a particular security in the market.

point A standard unit of value; for debt, typically, 1 percent of the loan amount. Points are considered prepaid interest and as such are income tax–deductible. Points paid on the principal mortgage are deductible the year paid; points paid upon refinance are deductible over the life of the loan. For investing, typically a unit value of $1.00 is used for quoting changes in stock prices. A bond point is equal to $10 (1 percent of $1,000 face value).

portfolio A combination of invested assets; the combined investment holdings of an investor.

positive cash flow When income exceeds expenses for the given period.

preferred stock A security that pays a fixed dividend and gives the owner a claim on corporate earnings and assets that is superior to those of common stockholders.

preliminary prospectus An abbreviated prospectus written by the issuer or underwriters that is distributed to the public while the issuer's registration is being reviewed by the SEC. It is issued in advance of an issue of new stock for the issuer to gauge the level of interest of the new issue. Commonly known as a "red herring," it has a warning written on the front of the prospectus in red ink, stating that the information in the document is incomplete or subject to change before the security is issued.

premium Price. As used in insurance, the cost of insurance coverage for a stipulated period of time. As used in investments, trading at a price in excess of par.

price-to-earnings ratio An analysis of a stock's price in relation to company earnings.

primary market The market involved with the trading of initial public offerings.

principal risk The risk of loss of principal.

prospectus The legal document that states the price of a new issue security, including information about the delivery date, underwriting spread, and other pertinent information that must be provided to any prospective investor before solicitation.

public offering An offering of common stock to the public by a corporation that is going public or offering additional shares of stock to the market.

public offering price Also referred to as "POP." The price of a mutual fund share to an investor, equal to the net asset value (NAV) plus the sales charge, if any.

qualified retirement plan An employer-sponsored retirement plan that receives privileged income tax treatment by the IRS. All employee contributions are made with before-tax dollars, meaning that income tax is not currently paid on any contributions. Employer contributions made to employee accounts are currently tax-deductible to the employer. Account earnings accumulate on a tax-deferred basis, meaning that no income tax is paid until withdrawals are taken from the account, usually during retirement. Withdrawals taken before age 59$^{1}/_{2}$ are subject to a 10 percent excise tax penalty in addition to regular income tax treatment, with limited exceptions.

quarterly report (Form 10-Q) A financial report of a publicly traded company that is required to be submitted on a quarterly basis for review by the SEC. It includes unaudited financial statements and other select management and operations information.

rate of return Investment growth plus income yield over a stated period of time. *See also* **return on investment.**

real property An asset that consists of land or buildings.

red herring *See* **preliminary prospectus.**

registered investment adviser (RIA) By law, an individual or business that receives compensation in any form for advice or services related to money, securities, or any financial product must register with the SEC. The SEC does not approve or disapprove of the registered investment adviser's professional knowledge or practice. This designation simply means that the person or business entity has complied with the law and registered with the SEC.

registered representative (RR) A person who is associated with an investment banking or securities business. As defined by the SEC, any financial services company employee who is not a principal of the company and who is not engaged in clerical or administrative services of the company is subject to registration and licensing requirements as a registered representative.

Regulation T A rule of the Federal Reserve Board that governs the extension of credit by broker/dealers to customers to purchase and carry securities.

reinvestment risk The risk that an investor faces when a bond is called or a fixed-income security matures. The risk is that interest rates that are available in the market at the time of reinvestment will be lower than the initial investment yield, resulting in a reduced yield on the investment and less interest income.

retained earnings After-tax income that is not distributed to shareholders. Net profits that are kept in the business after dividends are paid.

return on investment The total profit or loss resulting from a securities transaction, usually stated as an annual percentage rate. *See also* **rate of return**.

right A privilege that allows existing company shareholders to buy shares of a new issue of common stock before it is offered to the public, usually offered to shareholders in proportion to the number of shares already owned (to allow them to maintain their proportionate share of ownership in the company). Rights offerings are offered for a short time and expire worthless if not exercised.

ROI *See* **return on investment**.

RR *See* **registered representative**.

S&P 500 *See* **Standard & Poor Corporation**.

sales charge *See* **commission** or **12(b)1 fees**.

savings bonds *See* **U.S. savings bonds**.

secondary market In lending, a company that buys loans from lenders. Lenders often sell loans to secondary markets so that they can continually replenish their lending funds, which in turn get marketed to fixed-income investors. In investing, the purchase or sale of an investment that takes place after the primary offering.

sector investing A speculative investment approach that involves investing in specific sectors of the economy that are expected to outperform other market sectors.

sector rotation investing A speculative investment approach that involves investing in specific sectors of the economy that are expected to outperform other market sectors on a cyclical basis.

selling short   A highly aggressive strategy that involves selling a security that is not presently owned, in hopes that the value of the security will decline.

SEP IRA   A qualified retirement plan for a small business of 25 employees or fewer. Contributions to each employee's individual SEP-IRA account can be made by the employer on a tax-deductible basis. Employee contributions are made on a pretax basis, typically by payroll deduction, as a percentage of income. Assets accumulate on a tax-deferred basis. IRS limitations pertaining to early withdrawal penalties apply. *See* **qualified retirement plan.**

separate account   Accounts that are maintained by insurance companies, separate from the company's general account or operating accounts, specifically for the purpose of separately managing the invested assets of variable annuity and variable life insurance contracts.

share   A proportionate unit of ownership.

short   A term used to describe the act of selling a security not owned by the seller. *See also* **selling short.**

short selling   *See* **selling short.**

short-term capital gain   Capital gain on a security that was held for less than one year. Short-term capital gains are taxed as ordinary income. *See* **capital gain.**

simple interest   When interest is calculated using a simple method, it is calculated at the end of the period. To calculate the interest earned on $1,000 earning 6 percent in a year, simply multiply $1,000 by .06. The result is $60 interest earnings per year of simple interest. *See also* **compound interest.**

SIMPLE IRA   A qualified retirement account for small businesses or self-employed individuals. The employee can contribute a maximum of $6,000 per year on a before-tax basis; the employer can contribute up to 3 percent of employee compensation on a tax-deductible basis. Assets accumulate on a tax-deferred basis. IRS limitations pertaining to early withdrawal penalties apply. *See* **qualified retirement plan.**

Simplified Employee Pension Plan   *See also* **SEP IRA.**

small-cap companies   *See* **NASDAQ Small-Cap Market.**

spread   The difference between the bid price and the asking price.

Standard & Poor 500 Stock Index *See* **Standard & Poor Corporation.**

Standard & Poor Corporation A company that rates stocks and bonds according to investment risk. Also known for compiling the Standard & Poor Index, commonly known as the Standard & Poor 500 Index or the S&P 500 Index, which tracks 400 industrial stocks, 20 transportation stocks, 40 financial stocks, and 40 public utilities as a measurement of broad market strength.

stock An instrument that certifies a proportionate unit of ownership in a corporation. *See also* **common stock.**

stock dividend New shares of stock that are distributed to shareholders as a dividend. This can be in addition to a cash dividend or in lieu of a cash dividend. It can be stock of the dividend-issuing company or stock of another company, usually a subsidiary of the issuing company.

stock exchange A financial institution that provides a central location for the purchase and sale of securities.

stock market An organized marketplace where securities are bought and sold on behalf of investors.

stock split The division of outstanding shares of a corporation into a larger number of shares, without changing the total capitalization of the company or the proportionate ownership of the shareholders. For example, in a two-for-one split, each owner of 100 shares would receive an additional 100 shares. If the shares were worth $50 each before the split for a total value of $500, after the split, each share would be worth $25, for the same total value of $500.

stock symbol A unique combination of letters that is used for identifying a security on a stock exchange. Stock market information provided to the public typically uses the stock symbol in lieu of the full company name.

stop loss order An order given to a broker by an investor that establishes the sell price of a stock, protecting profits that have been made and limiting losses if the stock were to drop in price.

stop order *See* **stop loss order.**

street name Term given to securities that are held in the name of the broker on behalf of the investor, allowing for an easy transfer of shares. If stock certificates are physically held by the investor, to change hands, actual physical certificates must be changed.

strike price The price at which an option is exercised.

Student Aid Report The Student Aid Report (SAR) is received a couple of weeks after the Free Application for Federal Student Aid (FAFSA) is mailed to the processor. The SAR contains all the information provided on the FAFSA, messages from the processor, and some calculations. Upon receipt, the SAR should be reviewed to make sure that all of the information is correct.

Student Loan Marketing Association (SLMA)—A nonprofit organization that buys student loans from many lenders and packages the loans to students in an effort to help students consolidate their loans into a single, more affordable loan. The SLMA sells packaged student loan portfolios to investors as a fixed-income security. Also known as "Sallie Mae."

subordinated debt Debt that is in a lesser position in terms of security of principal. In the event of bankruptcy or liquidation, subordinated debt holders are paid after secured debtors.

surrender charge Also known as a contingent deferred sales charge (*see also* **CDSC**). Typically, this is a reducing charge over a limited period of years. The charge is imposed by the insurance company upon termination or surrender of a life insurance contract or annuity. This sales charge also could be imposed upon the surrender of B or C shares of mutual funds. Also known as a back-end load.

syndicate A group of investment banking firms formed to conduct an underwriting of a new security issue.

systematic risk The potential for a security to decrease in value simply because of a tendency for all securities of a similar type to move together. No investment strategy can eliminate systematic risk. *See also* **market risk**.

T-bill *See* **Treasury bill (T-bill)**.

T-bond *See* **Treasury bond**.

T-note *See* **Treasury note**.

tax basis *See* **adjusted basis**.

taxable income Net income that is taxed; for individuals, adjusted gross income, minus itemized deductions, minus personal exemptions equals taxable income.

"The Street" The New York Stock Exchange.

"The Curb" The American Stock Exchange.

ticker tape A tape that shows a consolidated reporting of securities prices from all American stock market exchanges.

time deposit A sum of money deposited in a bank that the customer agrees to not withdraw for a specified time or without notice.

timing *See* **market timing.**

Trail Commission *See* **12(b)1 fee.**

Treasury bill (T-bill) A type of simple-interest U.S. government security that matures in one year or less. Available maturities are 13-week, 26-week, or 52-week. They are sold at auction in a competitive bidding process. Interest payments on many debt instruments are tied to the T-bill rate. The investors who buy them are making a short-term loan to the federal government. The 52-week T-bill matures in one year, meaning that the investor gets all of the original investment, plus interest, one year following the original investment date. They are issued in denominations of $10,000 to $1,000,000 in $5,000 increments. T-bills are quoted at a discount from par. For example, a quote of 5.50 percent means that the bill is selling for 5½ percent less than its face value. A $10,000 52-week T-bill would sell for $9,450. A T-bill quote would read as follows: Maturity Apr 6, Bid 5.5%, ask 5.35%. The bid is higher than the ask because the buyer wants to improve the yield by buying at a deeper discount.

Treasury bond (T-bond) A simple-interest U.S. government security that pays interest every six months. T-bonds are sold in book-entry form only and are issued in denominations of $1,000 to $1,000,000. Maturities are 10 years or more. T-bonds are issued, quoted, and negotiated in $\frac{1}{32}$ of a percentage of $1,000 par value (Examples: $97^{24}/_{32}$ is equal to $97\frac{3}{4}$.) Bond quotes can also be written as 97-24 (24 referring to 32nds) or 97:24. A quote of 97.24 = $97 24/32 × $1,000 = $9775.

Treasury note (T-note) A simple-interest U.S. government security that pays interest every six months. They are issued only in book-entry form in denominations of $1,000 to $1,000,000. T-notes mature in 1 to 10 years. They are issued, quoted, and negotiated in 1/32nds of a percentage of $1,000 par value. (Examples: $97^{24}/_{32}$ is equal to $97\frac{3}{4}$.) T-note quotes can also be written as 97-24 (24 referring to 32nds) or 97:24. A quote of 97.24 = $97 24/32 × $1,000 = $9775.

triple witching day The last day that options, futures, and futures options trade before their expiration date.

underwriter An investment banker who works with an issuer of securities to help bring the offering to market.

Uniform Gift to Minors Act (UGMA)   A legislative act that allows for a gift of money or securities to be made to a minor and held in a custodial account that is managed by an adult for the child's benefit until the child reaches the age of majority.

Uniform Trust for Minors Act (UTMA)   A legislative act that has been enacted in some states that allows for a gift of money or securities to be made to a minor and held in a custodial account that is managed by an adult for the child's benefit until the child reaches a stated age, not necessarily the age of majority.

U.S. savings bonds   Bonds that are issued by the U.S. Department of the Treasury and backed by the full faith and credit of the United States government. *See also* **EE bonds** and **HH bonds.**

Value Line   An investment advisory service that rates the safety and projected price performance of hundreds of stocks.

variable annuity   An annuity contract that allows investment in any number of separate accounts during the accumulation phase and payout phase. Investment return will depend upon the performance of the separate account. During the payout phase, distribution payments are based upon the performance of separate accounts and actuarial assumptions. *See also* **fixed annuity, annuitant, accumulation phase, annuitize, payout phase,** and **separate account.**

venture capital   Capital that is invested in start-up business enterprises; a highly aggressive growth investment.

vesting   A term that is used regarding qualified retirement plan accounts; an ERISA guideline that requires that an employee be entitled to all retirement benefits upon leaving employment after a certain number of years of service.

vesting schedule   A schedule showing the number of years that an employee must work before being entitled to a percentage of or all retirement benefits upon termination or resignation from employment.

volume of shares   The number of shares traded on an exchange in a given period of time, typically quoted on a daily basis.

warrant   A security that gives the holder the right to purchase securities from the issuer of the warrant at a stipulated subscription price. Warrants are usually long-term instruments with maturities of one year or more.

wrap fee   A fee paid to a financial planner or account executive for services that are wrapped or bundled together, such as brokerage, advisory, investment management, and research services. The fee is usually paid as a percentage of assets under management.

yield   The rate of return on an investment, usually stated as an annual percentage rate. *See also* **current yield, nominal yield, yield to call,** and **yield to maturity.**

yield curve   Graph representing the yields of bonds in relation to their maturity dates.

yield to call (YTC)   The rate of return on a bond calculated to the earliest date that the bond could be called.

yield to maturity (YTM)   The rate of return on a bond calculated to its maturity date.

Index

K-L

N

O

P

Q

R

U

V

W–X